NeuroMastery

Retraining Your Brain to Conquer Anxiety, Fear, and Panic Attacks

Ugochukwu Uche MS., LPC

Copyright 2023 by Ugochukwu Uche

All rights reserved. This book or any portion thereof may not be reproduced or used in any manner whatsoever without the express written permission of the publisher except for the use of brief quotations in a book review.

ISBN: 979-8-35091-702-4 (print)
ISBN: 979-8-35091-703-1 (eBook)

TABLE OF CONTENTS

Introduction 1
    Understanding Anxiety, Fear, and Panic Attacks 1
    The Power of Neuroscience 2
    This is the Story of Lucy 3

Chapter 1: The Neuroscience of Anxiety, Fear, and Panic 5
    Anatomy of Anxiety: Amygdala, Prefrontal Cortex, and Hippocampus .. 5
    Neural Pathways: How Anxiety Travels Through Your Brain 7
    Neuroplasticity: The Brain's Ability to Change 8
    What's going on in Lucy's Brian? 10

Chapter 2: The Cycle of Fear and Panic.. 13
    Identifying Triggers 13
    The Fight, Flight, or Freeze Response 15
    The Feedback Loop of Fear 16
    Lucy Identifies Her Triggers and Breaks Her Cycle of Fear 21

Chapter 3: The Role of Thoughts and Beliefs.. 23
    How Your Thoughts Influence Your Brain 23
    The Cognitive Neuroscience of Beliefs 30
    Identifying and Changing Negative Thought Patterns 32
    Changing Lucy's Mind 34

Chapter 4: The Power of Mindfulness and Presence 37
    Neuroscientific Benefits of Mindfulness 37
    Mindfulness Techniques for Anxiety Management 39
    Cultivating Presence and Living in the Now 41
    Lucy Pays Attention 43

Chapter 5: Cognitive Behavioral Strategies for Anxiety Management 45
- *Understanding Cognitive Behavioral Therapy (CBT) 45*
- *Applying CBT Techniques to Anxiety, Fear, and Panic 47*
- *The Neuroscience Behind Why CBT Works 49*
- *Changing Lucy's Mind, Part II 51*

Chapter 6: Emotional Regulation and Self-Care 57
- *The Science of Emotional Regulation 57*
- *Effective Self-Care Strategies for Anxiety Relief 59*
- *Restoring Balance: Sleep, Nutrition, and Exercise 62*
- *Lucy Practices Self-Care 64*

Chapter 7: Techniques for Exposure and Desensitization 69
- *Understanding Exposure Therapy 69*
- *Systematic Desensitization 71*
- *The Neurobiology of Exposure and Desensitization 73*
- *Lucy, Slowly and Gradually Loses Her Fears 75*

Chapter 8: The Impact of Lifestyle on Anxiety and Fear 83
- *The Neuroscience of Exercise and Anxiety Management 83*
- *Nutrition and Mental Health 86*
- *The Role of Sleep in Anxiety Management 93*
- *Lucy Makes Lifestyle Changes 95*

Chapter 9: Building Resilience and Fostering Positive Change 97
- *Understanding Resilience from a Neuroscientific Perspective 97*
- *Strategies for Building Resilience 99*
- *Lucy Builds Resiliency 102*

Chapter 10: Creating Your Anxiety Management Plan 105
- *Implementing and Evaluating Your Plan 109*
- *Lucy's Treatment Plan 113*

Conclusion 117

BOOK SUMMARY

Anxiety, fear, and panic attacks can feel overwhelming and uncontrollable, but with the help of neuroscience, you can learn to understand and change your response to these emotions. *NeuroMastery: Retraining Your Brain to Conquer Anxiety, Fear, and Panic Attacks* delves into the intricate relationship between your brain and these feelings, providing actionable strategies rooted in neuroscience to empower you to take control.

Based on the latest research on cognitive neuroscience, and counseling psychology research, this book offers a comprehensive guide to reshaping your brain's response to anxiety, fear, and panic attacks. You will learn about the brain's anatomy, the path that stress takes through your brain, and how negative thought patterns contribute to anxiety and fear.

This book also introduces effective cognitive behavioral strategies, mindfulness techniques, and lifestyle modifications to manage anxiety. Learn how to face your fears through exposure and desensitization and discover how resilience and positive change can be nurtured by understanding and harnessing neuroplasticity.

NeuroMastery: Retraining Your Brain to Conquer Anxiety, Fear, and Panic Attacks is more than just a book—it is a roadmap to a calmer, more controlled, and resilient life.

INTRODUCTION

Understanding Anxiety, Fear, and Panic Attacks

Anxiety, fear, and panic attacks can profoundly impact the lives of those who experience them. They can disrupt everyday routines, influence relationships, hinder productivity, and lower quality of life. Understanding these conditions is the first step toward regaining control and restoring balance.

Anxiety is a natural response to stress and potential danger. It is characterized by unease, such as worry or fear, and it can be a normal and often healthy emotion. However, when feelings of intense fear or distress become overwhelming and start to affect daily life, it can manifest as an anxiety disorder.

In contrast, fear is an emotional response to a known or definite threat. It prepares the body for a fight-or-flight reaction—a set of changes in body functions that enhance the ability to confront or escape the threat. It is a primary survival mechanism for responding to a specific stimulus, such as pain or danger.

Panic attacks are sudden episodes of intense fear that trigger severe physical reactions when there is no real danger or apparent cause. They can be very frightening and may make you think you're having a heart attack, losing control, or even dying. They can occur unexpectedly, sometimes even during sleep.

These emotional experiences are intricately tied to the workings of our brains. We can gain invaluable insights into why they occur and how they affect our behavior through neuroscience. This understanding forms the foundation for effective intervention strategies for managing and overcoming anxiety, fear, and panic attacks.

The Power of Neuroscience

The human brain, with its complex networks of neurons and intricate pathways, is an astonishing wonder of nature. It is the command center for our body, influencing every aspect of our existence, from our thoughts and emotions to our behavior and physical health. Understanding our brains unlocks a vast potential for change and growth. This is where the power of neuroscience comes into play.

Neuroscience is the scientific study of the nervous system, focusing on the brain. This field brings together experts in biology, psychology, chemistry, physics, mathematics, and more to understand the most complex organ in the human body. The insights that neuroscience offers can help us grasp why we think, feel, and behave the way we do and how we can change these patterns when they become harmful.

One of the most exciting concepts in neuroscience is neuroplasticity—the brain's ability to change and adapt throughout an individual's life. This capacity allows us to learn new skills, recover from brain injuries, and adapt to new environments or experiences. Neuroplasticity offers hope for change in mental health, even in the face of debilitating conditions such as anxiety, fear, and panic attacks.

In this book, we will explore the power of neuroscience, as it applies to these conditions. We will delve into how anxiety, fear, and panic affect the brain and how the brain, in turn, influences these emotional states. We will also examine how our understanding of the brain can guide us toward techniques and interventions that harness the brain's plasticity to instigate change, allowing us to manage and ultimately conquer these conditions.

By illuminating the brain's inner workings, neuroscience enables us to devise strategies to reshape our neural pathways, allowing for healthier thought patterns, emotions, and behavior patterns. As we journey through this book, we will unravel the power of neuroscience and how it can be leveraged to overcome the struggles of anxiety, fear, and panic attacks. We will also explore how various scientifically backed techniques can help rewire our brain's response to stress and worry, providing a roadmap to improved mental health and well-being. By understanding our brain, we can find the path to its mastery. Welcome to your journey toward "NeuroMastery."

This is the Story of Lucy

In this book, to further assist your comprehension of how to retrain your brain, you will be introduced to the story of Lucy. Lucy, a twenty-six-year-old woman, came to therapy, seeking help with her issues with recurring panic attacks. According to Lucy, her panic attacks occurred mostly when she was driving. Occasionally, they occurred when she was a passenger in the front seat. Lucy was driven to therapy by her boyfriend; she reported that she rode in the backseat because she was afraid of experiencing another panic attack.

In the story of Lucy, you will follow at the end of each chapter about how she learns to overcome her issues with recurring panic attacks, fear of driving, and anxiety. Further, throughout the book, the concepts discussed about anxiety, fear, and panic and how to retrain your brain to become calmer and more relaxed, will be demonstrated in the story of Lucy.

CHAPTER 1

THE NEUROSCIENCE OF ANXIETY, FEAR, AND PANIC

Anatomy of Anxiety: Amygdala, Prefrontal Cortex, and Hippocampus

Anxiety is an emotional state experienced psychologically and has a solid biological basis. It results from complex brain interactions involving various structures and neural pathways. Three primary regions play critical roles in this process: the amygdala, the prefrontal cortex (PFC), and the hippocampus.

<u>The Amygdala</u>

Considered the fear center of the brain, the amygdala is a small, almond-shaped structure deep within the brain's temporal lobes. It is part of the limbic system, a group of structures involved in emotional processing. The amygdala plays a pivotal role in fear and anxiety by interpreting sensory information and initiating the body's response to danger. When we encounter a potential threat, the amygdala triggers physical and emotional responses—increased heart rate, shortness of breath, and feelings of fear and apprehension—that prepare us to react to the threat.

The Prefrontal Cortex

The prefrontal cortex (PFC), located in the frontal lobe, is responsible for higher-order cognitive functions like decision-making, planning, and regulating social behavior. It also plays a crucial role in managing emotional responses triggered by the amygdala. In situations of perceived danger, the PFC helps assess the actual risk and determine an appropriate response. It can also inhibit the amygdala's response, helping to control and lessen feelings of fear or anxiety. If functioning correctly, the PFC provides a "brake" for the fear response initiated by the amygdala.

The Hippocampus

The hippocampus, another part of the limbic system, is primarily responsible for memory formation. It helps store and retrieve memories related to fear and trauma. When a fearful or traumatic event occurs, the hippocampus is responsible for encoding this event into memory. During future situations that are similar to or associated with the original event, these memories are recalled, which can lead to feelings of anxiety.

In a well-functioning brain, these three structures work harmoniously to appropriately manage and respond to threats. However, in individuals with anxiety disorders, this process may be dysregulated. For example, an overactive amygdala may trigger an intense fear response to non-threatening stimuli. At the same time, an underactive PFC may struggle to regulate this response, leading to excessive and uncontrollable feelings of anxiety. Additionally, the hippocampus may retrieve distressing memories too readily, adding to these feelings.

In the following chapters, we will further explore these intricate interactions and how understanding these processes can help develop strategies to manage and mitigate anxiety. As we begin to comprehend the complex neurobiology of stress, we can better understand why we experience anxiety and how we can influence these underlying processes to manage it better.

Neural Pathways: How Anxiety Travels Through Your Brain

To understand the complex nature of anxiety, it's essential to examine the neural pathways, or circuits, that transmit anxiety signals through the brain. These networks of neurons, much like a highway system for information, play a crucial role in how we process and react to anxiety-provoking stimuli.

At the most basic level, when we encounter something that triggers anxiety, a sensory signal is sent to the thalamus, a structure that acts as the brain's sensory relay station. From the thalamus, the signal travels along two separate pathways.

<u>The Low Road and the High Road</u>

The first pathway, often called the "low road," is the quick but imprecise route. The signal is sent directly to the amygdala, triggering an immediate emotional response. This path allows us to react quickly to potential threats, even before we fully understand the danger. This route is responsible for our instinctual "jump" when we see a shadow in the corner of our vision or hear a sudden loud noise.

The second pathway, the "high road," takes a little longer but is more deliberate. Here, the signal is sent from the thalamus to the sensory cortex, where the threat is identified more accurately. From there, it goes to the hippocampus, which uses stored memories to add context to the situation, and then to the PFC, which evaluates the threat and decides how to respond. Finally, the signal is sent to the amygdala, which triggers an emotional response in line with the information received.

In a well-functioning brain, these two pathways work together to ensure we respond appropriately to threats. The low road allows for a rapid response, while the high road, although slower, provides a more accurate and nuanced reaction.

Dysregulation in Anxiety

However, in individuals who experience anxiety, these pathways may have an imbalance or dysregulation. The low road might be overly active, triggering strong emotional responses to harmless stimuli. Or the high road might not function optimally, leading to difficulties in correctly identifying and assessing threats.

Moreover, constant activation of these stress responses can lead to changes in these neural pathways. This can result in heightened sensitivity to stress and potential threats and contribute to the development and maintenance of anxiety disorders.

Understanding these neural pathways of anxiety is essential for managing it. We can work toward recalibrating these pathways through therapeutic techniques and interventions, reducing overreactions to harmless stimuli, and fostering healthier responses to stress. In the following sections, we will explore strategies grounded in neuroscience principles, paving the way for effective anxiety management.

Neuroplasticity: The Brain's Ability to Change

The human brain is an incredibly dynamic organ, possessing the remarkable ability to change and adapt throughout our lifetime. This capacity for change, known as neuroplasticity, provides a foundation for learning, memory, recovery from brain damage, and adaptation to new experiences.

Neuroplasticity represents the brain's ability to reorganize by forming new neural connections. These changes can occur at various levels, from individual neurons creating new links to frequent adjustments in the brain's neural pathways and networks.

Neuroplasticity is active throughout our lives, but 'it's particularly pronounced during the early stages of development, when the brain is still growing and forming significant connections. However, even in adulthood, our brain adapts and changes in response to our environment, behavior, emotions, and learning.

How Neuroplasticity Works

Neuroplasticity works through two primary processes: synaptic plasticity and neurogenesis.

Synaptic plasticity refers to the ability of connections, or synapses, between neurons to strengthen or weaken over time. This process is crucial for learning and memory. When we repeatedly practice a skill or recall a memory, the synaptic connections involved in that task become stronger, making it easier to perform that skill or remember that information in the future. This is often summed up with the phrase, "Neurons that fire together, wire together."

In contrast, neurogenesis involves the birth of new neurons, or nerve cells, in the brain. For a long time, humans were believed to be born with all the neurons they would ever have. However, more recent research has shown that new neurons can form in certain parts of the adult brain—most notably, the hippocampus, a region involved in learning and memory.

Neuroplasticity and Anxiety

In the context of anxiety, neuroplasticity offers a hopeful perspective. Just as unhealthy thought patterns and behaviors can change our brains in ways that contribute to stress, we can also harness neuroplasticity to reshape our brains in healthier directions.

Cognitive behavioral strategies, mindfulness, exposure therapy, and other interventions can all engage neuroplasticity to help reduce anxiety. By repeatedly engaging in these practices, we can help form new neural connections and pathways that support healthier responses to stress and fear.

The concept of neuroplasticity underlines that our brains are not static but dynamic and constantly changing. By understanding and leveraging this inherent plasticity, we can become active participants in reshaping our brains, promoting resilience and recovery, and ultimately mastering anxiety.

What's going on in Lucy's Brian?

The first thing the therapist did was determine when Lucy's panic attacks started and for how long they had been occurring. Lucy revealed that one day she was involved in a terrible car accident. She shared that she was cut off by a driver pulling out of a gas station, and when she swerved to miss him, she drove into a tree by the side of the road. She suffered a concussion and a broken forearm from the accident. She further shared that, following the accident, she began to experience recurring panic attacks, specifically while driving. She reports that the last time she experienced a panic attack, she was in the front seat of her mother's car. The anxiety around her next panic attack has become so profound that she has developed a fear of driving. After three months of suffering, she is now motivated to bring these panic attacks to an end and lose her fear of driving.

The human brain is an intricate system, a nexus of countless interconnected pathways, each having a particular function. To understand Lucy's experience, we need to explore how her brain is responding to driving following her traumatic car accident.

At the center of panic attacks is Lucy's amygdala, a part of the brain that plays a pivotal role in processing emotions, especially fear. When Lucy had her car accident, her brain was flooded with stress hormones that etched the incident into her memory. The vividness and emotional intensity of this memory primed her amygdala to be on high alert. Now, whenever Lucy is in a driving situation, her amygdala reacts as if she is in immediate danger, triggering a full-blown panic attack.

To better understand Lucy's fear and panic response, we must consider her brain's attempt to protect her from perceived danger. Every time she perceives a driving situation, her brain, more specifically the amygdala, recalls the trauma of the accident. The amygdala is the region of the brain responsible for emotional processing and threat detection.

Following the car accident, Lucy's brain associated driving with danger and potential harm. The amygdala's hyperactivation in response to this perceived threat initiates the "fight, flight, or freeze" response. This survival mechanism floods her body with adrenaline and other stress hormones, preparing her to confront or escape the perceived danger. This response manifests in physical symptoms, such as a racing heart, rapid breathing, sweating, trembling, and a strong urge to escape the situation, which collectively form what we recognize as a panic attack.

Furthermore, Lucy's PFC, the region of the brain involved in executive functions like decision-making and cognitive control over emotional reactions, tries to rationalize fear and inhibit the amygdala's response. However, when her anxiety spikes during driving, the emotional response from the amygdala can overwhelm the PFC's regulatory efforts, resulting in a panic attack.

Lucy's fear of future panic attacks—known as anticipatory anxiety—further exacerbates the situation. This fear can trigger the amygdala, causing another panic attack and creating a vicious cycle. It's as if her brain is stuck in a feedback loop where the fear of a panic attack triggers a panic attack, reinforcing the fear.

Moreover, the hippocampus, responsible for consolidating memories from short-term to long-term, plays a crucial role in Lucy's anxiety. It holds the traumatic memory of the accident and retrieves it when she's in similar contexts. The strength of this memory makes it easy to recall, amplifying her fear and anxiety about driving.

Hence, using cognitive behavioral strategies and exposure therapy, the therapy will focus on breaking this feedback loop of fear and helping Lucy's brain relearn that driving isn't a threat. This relearning will involve forming new, non-threatening associations with driving that can gradually overwrite the trauma response, helping Lucy regain control over her emotions and responses.

CHAPTER 2

THE CYCLE OF FEAR AND PANIC

Identifying Triggers

Fear and panic are closely linked to anxiety; like anxiety, they are not random occurrences. They are usually set off by specific triggers—elements or circumstances the brain has learned to associate with potential danger or discomfort. These triggers can be external, such as certain places or people, or internal, such as specific thoughts or physiological sensations. Identifying these triggers is crucial to understanding and managing fear and panic.

<u>The Cycle of Fear and Panic</u>

The cycle of fear and panic begins when a trigger sets off a fear response in the brain. This response is mediated largely by the amygdala, which signals the release of stress hormones like adrenaline and cortisol. These hormones prepare the body for the fight-or-flight response, leading to symptoms like a rapid heartbeat, quickened breathing, sweating, and trembling.

Once the immediate threat passes, the body is supposed to return to its normal state. However, for individuals prone to panic attacks or excessive fear responses, the high-stress hormones and the physical symptoms they produce can become triggers, creating a vicious cycle of fear and panic.

For example, someone might have a panic attack in a crowded mall. Afterward, they might begin to fear situations where escape could be difficult, leading them to avoid crowded places. The fear of another panic attack might trigger one, leading to an ongoing cycle of fear and avoidance.

Identifying Triggers

Identifying triggers involves close self-observation and possibly remembering when fear or panic episodes occur. What were you doing when it happened? Where were you? What were you thinking about? Were there any noticeable physical sensations?

This process might reveal specific triggers. For instance, you might notice that your fear spikes when you're in crowded places, during periods of high stress, or when you're reminded of past traumatic experiences. Sometimes, the triggers might not be obvious or internal, such as certain thought patterns or physical sensations.

Importance of Identifying Triggers

Understanding your triggers is essential to breaking the cycle of fear and panic. It allows you to anticipate potential fear or panic situations and develop coping strategies to manage them effectively. By recognizing these triggers, you can also work toward desensitizing your responses to them over time using therapeutic approaches like cognitive behavioral therapy (CBT) or exposure therapy.

By gaining insight into the cycle of fear and panic and the role of triggers, we can harness this knowledge to enact change.

The Fight, Flight, or Freeze Response

Humans, like all animals, are hard-wired for survival. When faced with perceived danger or threat, our bodies respond with the fight, flight, or freeze response. This first response prepares us to face the threat, escape it, or become immobilized.

Understanding the Fight, Flight, or Freeze Response

The fight, flight, or freeze response begins in the amygdala, the brain's alarm system. When a threat is detected, the amygdala sends a distress signal to the hypothalamus. Acting like a command center, the hypothalamus communicates with the rest of the body through the autonomic nervous system, which controls involuntary body functions.

The autonomic nervous system has two components: the sympathetic and parasympathetic nervous systems. The sympathetic nervous system triggers the fight-or-flight response, releasing adrenaline into the bloodstream. This leads to several physiological changes: heart rate and blood pressure increase, pupils dilate, muscles tense up, and non-emergency bodily processes, like digestion, slow down. These changes ready the body for action.

In contrast, the parasympathetic nervous system counteracts the sympathetic nervous system, promoting relaxation and recovery after the threat has passed. It lowers the heart rate, reduces blood pressure, and resumes normal bodily functions.

The freeze response, often less discussed, is another key aspect of this survival mechanism. Sometimes, individuals may find themselves frozen in place instead of fighting or fleeing. This reaction could be viewed as a form of self-protection. One might avoid becoming a target by remaining still and not attracting attention.

<u>The Fight, Flight, or Freeze Response in Anxiety</u>

In individuals with anxiety disorders, the fight, flight, or freeze response may be triggered too easily, often in response to perceived threats that are not dangerous. For example, someone with social anxiety might experience a fight-or-flight response when asked to speak in public, even though this situation does not pose a physical threat.

The repeated triggering of the fight, flight, or freeze response can lead to physical and emotional exhaustion, contributing to symptoms of anxiety and panic disorders. It can also create a vicious cycle, as the physical sensations associated with this response (e.g., rapid heart rate, shortness of breath) can become triggers themselves, causing further anxiety and fear.

<u>Regulating the Response</u>

Understanding the fight, flight, or freeze response can be crucial to managing anxiety. By recognizing these responses for what they are—normal, adaptive reactions to perceived threats—we can start de-escalating the fear and anxiety associated with them.

The Feedback Loop of Fear

Fear is not just an emotion; it's a complex interaction between our brains and bodies. It's not always harmful—in fact, fear is crucial for survival, alerting us to potential danger. But for individuals with anxiety disorders, fear can become a recurring, debilitating experience, transforming delicate situations into perceived threats. This is often due to what's known as the feedback loop of fear.

Understanding the Feedback Loop of Fear

The feedback loop of fear starts with an initial trigger—an event, situation, or even a thought that the brain interprets as threatening. This trigger activates the amygdala, the brain's alarm center, sparking a cascade of physiological responses—the fight, flight, or freeze response. Heart and breathing rates increase, muscles tense up, and the body is alert.

In a person with anxiety disorder, these physiological responses can become a source of fear. For example, a rapid heartbeat might be interpreted as a sign of a heart attack, leading to more anxiety and heightened physical symptoms. This increased fear then acts as a new trigger, leading to a stronger fight-or-flight response and thus creating a self-perpetuating cycle of fear and anxiety.

Cognitive Distortions and the Feedback Loop

The feedback loop of fear is also closely connected to cognitive distortions—irrational thought patterns that distort reality. These might include catastrophizing (believing the worst will happen), overgeneralizing (believing that because something bad happened once, it will always happen), or black-and-white thinking (viewing things in absolute, all-or-nothing terms).

Cognitive distortions are biased perspectives we take on ourselves and the world around us. They are irrational thoughts and beliefs that we unknowingly reinforce over time. These patterns and systems of thought are often subtle, making them hard to identify. However, they can lead to a consistent and biased way of thinking that's often not in line with reality. Cognitive distortions can contribute to mental health disorders like anxiety, depression, and other mood disorders.

Here are some of the most common types of cognitive distortions:

All-or-Nothing Thinking (Polarized Thinking): You see things as black-and-white categories. If a situation falls short of perfection, you see it as a failure.

Overgeneralization: You perceive a global pattern of negatives based on a single incident. "This always happens to me. I seem to fail at many things."

Filtering (Mental Filter): You focus on the negative details of a situation and filter out all the positive aspects. A single piece can change your view of the whole situation.

Disqualifying the Positive: You reject positive experiences by insisting they "don't count" for some reason. You maintain a negative belief that is contradicted by your everyday experiences.

Jumping to Conclusions: You make negative interpretations even though no definitive facts convincingly support your conclusion. This can manifest as "mind reading" (assuming the thoughts and intentions of others) or "fortune-telling" (anticipating the worst).

Magnification (Catastrophizing) or Minimization: You exaggerate the importance of things (such as your goof-up or someone else's achievement) or you inappropriately shrink things until they appear tiny (your desirable qualities or the other fellow's imperfections).

Emotional Reasoning: You assume that your negative emotions necessarily reflect how things are: "I feel it. Therefore, it must be true."

Should Statements: You try to motivate yourself with should and shouldn't, as if you must be whipped and punished before being expected to do anything. "Musts" and "oughts" are also offenders. The emotional consequence is guilt.

Labeling and Mislabeling: This is an extreme form of overgeneralization. Instead of describing your error, you attach a negative label to yourself: "I'm a loser." Mislabeling involves describing an event with language that is highly colored and emotionally loaded.

Personalization: You see yourself as the cause of some negative external event for which you are not primarily responsible.

These cognitive distortions can intensify fear and anxiety, fueling the feedback loop. For instance, if you're prone to catastrophizing, you might interpret physical signs of stress like a rapid heartbeat or shortness of breath as signals of impending doom, spiraling into more intense fear and stronger physical symptoms.

Breaking the Feedback Loop

The good news is that the feedback loop of fear can be interrupted. Strategies involve both managing the physical symptoms of anxiety and addressing the cognitive distortions that contribute to the cycle.

Cognitive behavioral therapy (CBT): CBT can help individuals recognize and challenge their cognitive distortions, providing a more realistic perspective.

Mindfulness and Relaxation Techniques: Practices like deep breathing, progressive muscle relaxation, and mindfulness meditation can help lower the physiological response to fear.

Exposure Therapy: Gradually exposing oneself to fear triggers in a controlled, safe environment can help decrease the sensitivity over time, leading to desensitization.

By understanding the feedback loop of fear and learning how to interrupt it, we can retake control over our fear and anxiety responses, effectively breaking the cycle.

Examining the feedback loop of fear and anxiety is crucial in understanding the neurobiology of fear and anxiety. This self-perpetuating cycle can amplify anxiety and make it harder to manage. This feedback loop can often underpin chronic anxiety disorders, making everyday situations feel overwhelmingly threatening.

The Feedback Loop Explained

The feedback loop of fear begins with a trigger—a situation, thought, or sensation perceived as threatening. This trigger activates the amygdala, leading to a fight, flight, or freeze response, which involves various physiological changes such as increased heart rate, rapid breathing, and heightened alertness.

For individuals with anxiety, these physiological changes can become triggers themselves. For instance, a rapid heart rate might be interpreted as a sign of impending danger, increasing fear and anxiety and intensifying the physiological response. This creates a feedback loop: fear leads to physical symptoms, which trigger more fear, more intense symptoms, and so forth.

The Role of Perception

A key aspect of the feedback loop of fear is perception. Our brain's interpretation of a situation, thought, or sensation can determine whether or not it triggers a fear response. For instance, someone without anxiety might interpret a rapid heart rate as a normal response to stress. In contrast, someone with anxiety might interpret it as a sign of a heart attack, leading to increased fear and anxiety.

This is where cognitive processes come into play. Our thoughts and beliefs about a situation can fuel or dampen our fear response. Negative, catastrophic thinking can amplify fear, while realistic, rational thinking can help manage it.

Breaking the Feedback Loop

Breaking the feedback loop of fear involves changing our physiological responses to fear triggers and modifying our perceptions of these triggers. This can be achieved through various neuroscience-based techniques, such as:

Cognitive Behavioral Therapy (CBT): This therapy can help individuals challenge and change negative thought patterns that contribute to the feedback loop of fear.

Mindfulness and Relaxation Techniques: These can help reduce the physiological response to fear, interrupting the feedback loop. Techniques include deep breathing, progressive muscle relaxation, and mindfulness meditation.

Exposure Therapy: Gradually and repeatedly exposing oneself to fear triggers in a safe environment can help desensitize the fear response over time.

By understanding the feedback loop of fear and learning to interrupt it, we can regain control over our fear response and reduce anxiety.

Lucy Identifies Her Triggers and Breaks Her Cycle of Fear

To address Lucy's recurring panic attacks, the therapist sought to understand her triggers. In therapy, triggers are experiences that stimulate a memory or reminder of a past traumatic event. For Lucy, driving and being in the front passenger seat were clear triggers directly linked to her traumatic car accident.

Through patient dialogue and reflection, the therapist helped Lucy identify subtler triggers that were less obvious. These could be anything from the sound of a car's engine revving to the sight of a tree by the roadside or even the smell of gasoline. By recognizing these triggers, she could better anticipate and manage her panic responses, an important step in breaking the feedback loop of fear.

The feedback loop of fear is a term used to describe how fear can amplify itself in a cyclical pattern. In Lucy's case, her fear of driving and fear of experiencing a panic attack became intertwined. When she would think about driving, she would anticipate a panic attack, which, in turn, would cause anxiety and fear, which then could trigger a panic attack. This cycle repeated and amplified each time she was confronted with a driving scenario, creating a self-perpetuating cycle of fear and panic attacks.

The fight, flight, or freeze response is a primal physiological reaction to a perceived threat or danger. When Lucy is exposed to triggers related to driving, her brain perceives them as a threat. It signals her body to prepare for immediate action: to either confront the danger (fight), escape the danger (flight), or become immobilized by it (freeze). She often freezes (riding in the backseat instead of driving) or flees (avoiding driving altogether).

The therapist used CBT to disrupt this cycle and response. The therapist did this by guiding Lucy to question and challenge her fear-based thoughts. They also worked on developing coping mechanisms, like controlled breathing and grounding techniques, to calm her body's panic response and help her regain control. Moreover, through systematic and controlled exposure to her triggers, she could slowly desensitize her reaction to them, gradually reducing the intensity of her fight, flight, or freeze response.

CHAPTER 3

THE ROLE OF THOUGHTS AND BELIEFS

How Your Thoughts Influence Your Brain

Our thoughts significantly influence the physical structure and function of our brains. This remarkable concept reveals the power of the mind to shape our brains, behaviors, and overall well-being.

<u>The Neurobiology of Thoughts</u>

Every thought we have triggered a cascade of biochemical processes in our brains. Thoughts activate brain cells, or neurons, which release neurotransmitters. These neurotransmitters communicate with other neurons, leading to electrical signals that travel throughout the brain.

The human brain is a complex network of neurons (nerve cells) that communicate with each other via electrical signals. This neuronal communication forms the basis for our thoughts, emotions, behaviors, and perceptions.

Here's a simplified explanation of how this works:

1. Neurons and Electrical Signals:

   Neurons have a cell body and numerous extensions called dendrites and axons. Dendrites receive information from other neurons, while axons send information out. When a neuron receives another signal, it generates an electrical impulse. This electrical impulse travels through the dendrites, the cell body, and down the axon.

2. The Role of Synapses:

   At the end of the axon, the electrical signal reaches a structure called a synapse, which is a tiny gap between the end of one neuron (the presynaptic neuron) and the dendrite of another neuron (the postsynaptic neuron).

3. The Conversion of Electrical Signals to Chemical Signals:

   When the electrical signal reaches the synapse, it triggers the release of neurotransmitters, which are chemical messengers. These neurotransmitters cross the synaptic gap and bind to receptors on the postsynaptic neuron. This binding can either stimulate the postsynaptic neuron to generate its electrical signal or inhibit the postsynaptic neuron from generating a signal.

4. The Generation of Thoughts:

   Our thoughts arise from the complex interplay of electrical and chemical signals in vast networks of neurons. Different studies and mental states involve different patterns of neuronal activity. For instance, other parts of the brain are involved in various thought processes—the frontal lobes are involved in planning and decision-making, the limbic system is involved in emotional processing, and the hippocampus is involved in memory formation and retrieval.

In essence, every thought you have corresponds to a specific pattern of neuronal activity. This means that your thoughts are both the result of and an influence on your brain's electrical activity.

Thoughts and Brain Structure

The concept of neuroplasticity illustrates how thoughts can shape the brain's structure. Neuroplasticity refers to the brain's ability to reorganize itself by forming new neural connections throughout life. Repeated thoughts and behaviors can change the brain's structure and function.

Every thought we have creates a pattern of neuronal activation in the brain. This activation pattern travels along certain pathways called neural networks. When we repeatedly have the same thought, the neurons in that network fire together, strengthening their connections. This is often summarized by the phrase, "Neurons that fire together, wire together."

Over time, repeated thought patterns can physically change the structure of these networks. For instance, frequently used neural pathways become more efficient and connections become stronger and more numerous, while less frequently used pathways can weaken.

The Influence of Thoughts on Brain Structure

This is a bidirectional relationship, meaning that while our thoughts shape our brain structure, our brain structure also influences our thoughts. For instance, areas of the brain involved in positive emotions, like the left PFC, tend to be more developed in individuals who habitually think positive thoughts. In contrast, individuals who frequently experience stress or negative thoughts may have a more reactive amygdala, a part of the brain involved in fear and anxiety.

Thoughts, Behavior, and Brain Structure

Our thoughts not only influence our brain structure but also guide our behaviors. And our behaviors can further influence our brain structure. For example, we can form and strengthen new neural pathways in the brain by adopting new behaviors in response to our thoughts (such as practicing mindfulness or learning a new skill).

Neuroplasticity and Change

The neuroplastic nature of our brains means that change is possible. Even if negative or unhelpful thought patterns have led to certain patterns in our brain structure, we can reshape those patterns through interventions like CBT, mindfulness, and other strategies. By cultivating positive, adaptive thoughts, we can make physical changes in our brains that support mental well-being and resilience.

So, the structure of our brain is not a fixed entity but a dynamic one, continuously changing in response to our thoughts, experiences, and actions. Understanding this can empower us to shape our brains in ways that support our mental health and overall well-being.

Thoughts, Emotions, and the Brain

Our thoughts also influence the brain through their impact on our emotions. Emotional responses are associated with activating certain brain parts, such as the amygdala, which plays a key role in fear and anxiety, and the PFC, which is involved in higher cognitive functions and emotion regulation.

Negative thoughts can trigger stress responses in the brain, activating the fight-or-flight response and releasing stress hormones like cortisol. On the other hand, positive reviews can stimulate brain reward pathways, releasing feel-good neurotransmitters like dopamine.

The interplay between thoughts, emotions, and the brain is complex and nuanced. Thoughts and emotions are both products of brain activity, yet they also have the power to influence how the brain functions and even its structure over time.

Thoughts and the Brain

Thoughts are the product of complex interactions between different regions of the brain. For example, the PFC, the brain's executive center, is involved in planning, decision-making, and moderating social behavior. The temporal lobe is linked to the formation and retrieval of memories. The parietal lobe plays a role in sensory information processing and spatial orientation.

When we have a thought, it triggers a pattern of neuronal activity across these various brain areas. Over time, repeated studies can strengthen the connections within these neural networks, shaping the brain's structure and function in a process known as neuroplasticity.

Emotions and the Brain

Emotions, like thoughts, arise from the activity of specific brain regions and networks. The limbic system, which includes structures such as the amygdala, the hippocampus, and the hypothalamus, plays a crucial role in emotional processing.

For example, the amygdala is essential for emotional responses such as fear and anger. While mostly associated with memory, the hippocampus plays a role in attaching emotions to these memories. The hypothalamus controls the physiological aspects of emotions, such as heart rate and adrenaline release.

The Interaction of Thoughts and Emotions

Thoughts and emotions are closely intertwined and can influence each other. For instance, a negative thought (*I can't do anything right*) can trigger negative emotions (such as sadness or frustration), while experiencing fear can lead to fearful thoughts (*I am in danger*).

Cognitive theories suggest that it's not the events that upset us but the meanings we give to them. So, by changing our thought patterns (cognitive restructuring), we can also change our emotional responses.

Cognitive Behavioral Therapy (CBT)

One practical application of this understanding is CBT, a form of psychological treatment that helps people recognize and change dysfunctional thought patterns that lead to negative emotions and behaviors. By reshaping these thought patterns, CBT can significantly improve mood, anxiety, and the overall quality of life.

The brain is the biological substrate where thoughts and emotions arise and interact. Yet, thoughts and feelings can also shape our neurobiology through their effects on the brain, highlighting the dynamic interplay between mind and brain.

Harnessing the Power of Thoughts

Harnessing the power of thoughts can be transformative for our mental health, behaviors, and overall quality of life. Understanding and influencing our thought processes can promote healthier brain function, reduce stress, and improve our emotional well-being. Here are several ways we can leverage the power of our thoughts:

1. Cognitive Behavioral Therapy (CBT):

   Cognitive behavioral therapy is a form of psychological treatment that's been extensively researched and is highly effective in treating various disorders, including depression, anxiety, and PTSD. Cognitive behavioral therapy identifies and changes harmful thought patterns, teaching individuals to challenge their cognitive distortions and reframe negative thinking.

2. Mindfulness and Meditation:

   Mindfulness involves focusing on the present moment and accepting it without judgment. Regular mindfulness practice can change the brain's structure and function, improve concentration, reduce stress, and promote emotional well-being. For example, mindfulness-based cognitive therapy (MBCT) combines mindfulness techniques with CBT to help prevent depression relapse.

3. Positive Thinking and Optimism:

   Research shows an optimistic outlook can provide numerous health benefits, including improved mood, a longer lifespan, and better physical health. It's not about ignoring the negative aspects of life but about trying to see challenges from a more positive perspective.

4. Visualization:

   Visualization, or mental imagery, is a technique where you imagine yourself in a specific situation, performing a particular task, or achieving a certain goal. Athletes often use this technique to enhance their performance. Visualization can also support cognitive restructuring, allowing you to 'practice' positive thinking and behaviors.

5. Self-Affirmations:

   Positive affirmations can help you challenge and overcome self-sabotaging and negative thoughts. When you repeat them often and believe in them, you can start to make positive changes in your life.

6. Lifelong Learning and Cognitive Stimulation:

    Keeping your mind active through lifelong learning, puzzles, reading, and other cognitive stimulation can promote healthier brain function and slow cognitive decline.

7. Neurofeedback:

    Neurofeedback uses real-time displays of brain activity—most commonly electroencephalography (EEG)—to teach self-regulation of brain function. This can be used to train the brain to change certain thought patterns.

Remember, changing thought patterns is a process and takes time. Be patient and consider seeking help from a mental health professional if you find the process overwhelming or if you are dealing with mental health disorders. They can provide tools and techniques tailored to your needs and situation.

The Cognitive Neuroscience of Beliefs

Beliefs are fundamental to human cognition and behavior as convictions or acceptances that certain things are true or real. They guide our understanding of the world, our decisions, and our actions, and they shape our emotional responses. The cognitive neuroscience of beliefs is a field of study that investigates the underlying neural mechanisms and processes that give rise to and shape our beliefs.

Formation of Beliefs

The formation of beliefs involves numerous cognitive processes, including perception, memory, judgment, and decision-making. Each of these cognitive processes is associated with particular brain regions and networks.

Perception and Belief: Our beliefs often begin with sensory perceptions of the world around us. These perceptions are processed in the brain's sensory cortices and interpreted in areas such as the parietal and temporal lobes.

Memory and Belief: Our memories play a crucial role in belief formation. Our beliefs are often based on what we remember about our past experiences and the information we've learned. The hippocampus and surrounding medial temporal lobe structures are integral to memory and, therefore, the formation and maintenance of our beliefs.

Judgment and Decision-Making: The frontal lobes, particularly the PFC, play a key role in judgment and decision-making—processes crucial for belief formation. The PFC helps us evaluate evidence, make predictions, and decide what we believe to be true.

Confirmation Bias

The brain is predisposed to pay more attention to information that aligns with our existing beliefs, a phenomenon known as confirmation bias. This bias helps to reduce cognitive dissonance (the discomfort experienced when we have conflicting beliefs or when our beliefs conflict with our actions), thereby maintaining a consistent belief system.

Neuroscience research has shown that when people encounter information that aligns with their beliefs, the brain releases dopamine, a neurotransmitter associated with pleasure and reward. This makes the assimilation of belief-confirming information pleasurable and motivates individuals to seek out such information.

Beliefs and Emotions

Our beliefs and emotions are deeply intertwined. The limbic system, including the amygdala and insula, plays a significant role in how emotions can shape our beliefs. We're more likely to form strong beliefs when strong emotions are involved. This is why beliefs tied to emotional events or experiences are often more robust and resistant to change.

Changing Beliefs

Changing beliefs can be difficult because they're often closely tied to our identities and worldviews. However, presenting new information or evidence, especially in a way that's consistent with an individual's values and in a supportive, non-threatening context, can lead to belief updating. This cognitive flexibility is associated with higher activity in the prefrontal cortex.

Understanding the cognitive neuroscience of beliefs provides insights into human cognition and behavior and has implications for fields like education, psychology, and politics. It informs strategies for teaching, persuasion, conflict resolution, and behavior change. As our understanding of the brain advances, so will our understanding of the complex neural processes that shape our beliefs.

Identifying and Changing Negative Thought Patterns

Understanding and changing negative and anxious thought patterns is a key goal in many types of psychotherapy, and neuroscience provides powerful insights into how we can do this effectively. The first step is to identify these thought patterns, and the second is to use techniques to change them.

Identifying Negative and Anxious Thought Patterns

Negative and anxious thought patterns often arise from cognitive distortions and biased perspectives on us and our world. They are usually negative and tend to amplify feelings of anxiety, depression, and stress. Common cognitive distortions include:

Catastrophizing: Expecting the worst-case scenario to happen.

Overgeneralization: Making broad interpretations from a single or few events.

All-or-Nothing Thinking: Viewing situations in only two categories instead of on a continuum.

Personalization: Blaming yourself for circumstances beyond your control.

Neuroscience has shown us that these thought patterns are associated with certain brain activity patterns. For example, anxiety and negative thinking have been linked to increased activity in the amygdala, the brain's fear center, and decreased activity in the PFC, which is involved in executive functions like decision-making and emotion regulation.

<u>Changing Negative and Anxious Thought Patterns</u>

Neuroplasticity, the brain's ability to change and adapt, allows us to break these negative and anxious thought patterns and form new, healthier ones. Here's how you can do this:

Cognitive Behavioral Therapy (CBT): This therapy is based on the idea that our thoughts, feelings, and behaviors are interconnected and that we can improve our mental health by changing maladaptive thoughts. In CBT, you'll work to identify your cognitive distortions, challenge their validity, and replace them with more realistic and balanced thoughts.

Mindfulness and Meditation: These practices can help you become more aware of your thought patterns, create a space between your thoughts and reactions, and reduce anxiety and stress. Over time, mindfulness can change the structure and function of the brain in ways that promote better mental health.

Neurofeedback: In neurofeedback sessions, the individual's brain automatically adjusts to its brain waves. It brings abnormally fast or slow brain waves back to normal wavelengths. This is based on feedback from the

EEG. Research has shown that neurofeedback can be beneficial in reducing symptoms of anxiety and depression.

Positive Psychology Interventions: Techniques such as gratitude journaling, savoring positive experiences, and practicing kindness can help shift your focus from negative to positive, retraining your brain to pay more attention to positive information.

Remember, changing thought patterns takes time and practice, so be patient. If you're struggling, consider seeking help from a mental health professional. They can guide you through these strategies and provide support along the way.

Changing Lucy's Mind

Thoughts play a crucial role in the wiring of our brains, thereby influencing brain functions. They serve as the catalysts that shape our emotions and behaviors, thus impacting how our brain reacts to different situations.

In Lucy's case, her traumatic car accident prompted a series of negative thoughts about driving. Thoughts such as *Driving is dangerous* or *I'll have a panic attack if I get in the driver's seat* were etched into her cognitive processes. These thoughts sparked fear and anxiety, triggering her amygdala, the brain's emotional center. This led to the release of stress hormones like adrenaline and cortisol, causing physical symptoms of panic attacks such as increased heart rate, rapid breathing, and sweating.

Furthermore, these negative thoughts reinforced the neural pathways associated with fear and panic, strengthening them with each panic episode. This is the "neurons that fire together, wire together" principle of neuroscience, also known as Hebbian theory. The more Lucy entertained these negative thoughts, the stronger these fear-based pathways became and the more prone she was to panic attacks.

To help Lucy change her negative thought patterns, the therapist employed a cognitive behavioral technique called cognitive restructuring. This involved identifying and challenging Lucy's irrational and fear-based thoughts. By asking questions such as "What is the evidence for and against this thought?" or "Is there a more positive and realistic way to view this situation?", the therapist guided Lucy to see that her thoughts were not factual truths but subjective interpretations.

They also worked on teaching Lucy to recognize cognitive distortions, which are skewed perceptions of reality often rooted in negative thinking. These could include "catastrophizing" (expecting the worst-case scenario) or "over-generalization" (viewing a single negative event as a never-ending pattern of defeat). Recognizing these distortions allowed Lucy to see her thoughts for what they were—distorted interpretations rather than concrete truths.

The therapist then encouraged Lucy to replace these negative thoughts with more realistic and positive ones. For example, instead of thinking, *I will have a panic attack if I drive,* Lucy was guided to think, *It's possible I might feel anxious, but I have the tools to manage my anxiety.*

Through persistent cognitive restructuring, Lucy gradually managed to weaken the neural pathways associated with fear and strengthen those associated with positive, rational thoughts. As she learned to perceive driving not as a threat but as a routine activity, her amygdala was less and less triggered, leading to a decrease in her panic responses. With time and practice, Lucy was able to regain control over her thoughts, ultimately mastering her fear of driving and her panic attacks.

CHAPTER 4

THE POWER OF MINDFULNESS AND PRESENCE

Neuroscientific Benefits of Mindfulness

Mindfulness is a mental state achieved by focusing on the present moment while calmly acknowledging and accepting one's feelings, thoughts, and bodily sensations. Originally rooted in Buddhist meditation practices, it has been popularized in both psychological therapies and general wellness practices in the Western world.

There are two key components of mindfulness:

Attention Regulation: This focuses on the immediate experience, whether your breath, bodily sensations, thoughts, emotions, or an aspect of the environment. The aim is to continually bring your attention back to the present moment, even when your mind wanders. This helps to strengthen your attention muscle, so to speak, increasing your ability to concentrate and focus.

Acceptance: This is about observing your experience without judgment. Instead of labeling certain thoughts or feelings as good or bad, you notice them for what they are. This doesn't mean you have to like or agree with everything that happens, but simply that you recognize it as part of your current reality.

Mindfulness can be practiced formally, such as during meditation, where one might focus on their breath, bodily sensations, or sounds around them. It can also be practiced informally by bringing awareness to everyday activities like eating, walking, or washing dishes.

Practicing mindfulness has numerous benefits. It can help reduce stress, anxiety, and negative mood states. It can improve focus and cognitive flexibility, enhance relationship satisfaction, increase resilience to challenging life events, and improve overall well-being. While it's simple in concept, like any skill, mindfulness takes practice to cultivate.

Furthermore, the benefits of mindfulness are underpinned by neuroscientific changes in the brain. Some of these changes include:

Enhanced Prefrontal Cortex Activity: The PFC is associated with executive functions such as decision-making, attention, and self-regulation. Regular mindfulness practice has been linked to increased activity in the PFC, which can enhance these cognitive functions. This can result in better concentration, improved emotional regulation, and more effective stress management.

Reduced Amygdala Activity: The amygdala is the brain's fear center and plays a key role in our stress response. Research has shown that mindfulness can decrease amygdala activity and the size of the amygdala, reducing emotional reactivity and anxiety.

Changes in the Default Mode Network (DMN): The DMN, which includes the medial PFC and the posterior cingulate cortex, is active when our minds are at rest and not focused on the outside world and is often involved in mind-wandering and ruminative thoughts. Mindfulness has been shown to reduce activity in the DMN, which can help reduce rumination and improve focus.

Increased Hippocampus Volume: The hippocampus is crucial for learning and memory. Studies have shown that mindfulness practices can increase the hippocampus's volume, enhancing memory and learning capacity.

Enhanced Connectivity Between Brain Regions: Mindfulness has been found to improve functional connectivity between different brain regions. This enhanced connectivity can lead to more efficient information processing and better emotional and cognitive information integration.

Promotion of Neuroplasticity: Neuroplasticity refers to the brain's ability to form and reorganize synaptic connections in response to learning or experience. Mindfulness promotes neuroplasticity, allowing the brain to change and adapt, enhancing cognitive flexibility and resilience to stress.

The neuroscientific benefits of mindfulness contribute to its positive effects on mental health and well-being. These benefits can be accessed through various mindfulness-based practices, such as mindfulness-based stress reduction (MBSR), mindfulness-based cognitive therapy (MBCT), yoga, tai chi, and meditation.

Mindfulness Techniques for Anxiety Management

Mindfulness is a powerful tool for managing anxiety. It involves paying attention to the present moment without judgment, which can help break the cycle of anxiety-inducing thoughts and physical sensations. Here are a few mindfulness techniques specifically designed to help manage anxiety:

Mindful Breathing:

Mindful breathing is one of the simplest ways to achieve mindfulness. The aim is to focus on your breath, noticing each inhalation and exhalation. This focus can slow down your overall thought process and reduce anxiety. Here's a simple method:

- Sit comfortably, close your eyes, and take a few moments to settle.
- Breathe normally and focus on your breath entering and leaving your body.
- If your mind wanders, notice where it goes, and then gently bring your attention back to your breath.

Body Scan:

A body scan involves paying attention to different body parts, from your toes to your head, and can effectively relieve anxiety. Here's a simple method:

Lie down or sit comfortably, close your eyes, and start by taking a few deep breaths. Begin focusing on your feet, noticing any sensations there. Slowly move your attention up your body—to your legs, abdomen, arms, and so forth—until you reach the top of your head.

If you notice any tension or discomfort in any part of your body, try to breathe into it and allow it to release.

Mindfulness Meditation:

Mindfulness meditation is a more formal practice where you set aside a specific time (fifteen minutes or more) to cultivate mindfulness. It often combines the techniques above and can include guided meditations.

Mindful Observing:

Choose an object in your visual field (a flower, a piece of art, or even your hand) and observe it as if you're seeing it for the first time. Notice its colors, shapes, texture, and other attributes. This can help ground you in the present and take your mind away from anxious thoughts.

Loving-Kindness Meditation:

This is a mindfulness method that promotes compassion toward yourself and others. It involves silently repeating phrases of goodwill for yourself and others, such as "May I be safe. May I be happy? May I be healthy? May I live with ease?"

Mindful Eating:

This involves paying attention to the process of eating, including the taste, smell, and texture of food and your body's hunger and fullness cues. This can help you enjoy the process of eating and distract you from anxiety.

Mindful Walking:

This involves paying attention to the physical act of walking, noticing the sensation of your feet touching the ground, the rhythm of your breath while walking, and the feeling of the wind against your skin.

Remember, mindfulness takes practice. Start with a few minutes each day and gradually increase your time. With patience and persistence, these techniques can be powerful tools for anxiety management.

Cultivating Presence and Living in the Now

Anxiety, fear, and panic are often the result of focusing too much on past experiences or future possibilities rather than being present in the current moment. Cultivating presence and living in the now can help shift your focus away from these stressors and alleviate these feelings. Here are some strategies to help you develop a company and live more fully in the now:

Practice Mindfulness:

Mindfulness is the act of deliberately focusing on the present moment in a nonjudgmental way. By practicing mindfulness, you can become more aware of your thoughts, feelings, and sensations as they occur and accept them without trying to change them or react to them. This can include mindfulness meditation, mindful eating, or simply taking a moment to breathe and observe your surroundings.

Single-Tasking:

In our modern world, multitasking is often the norm. However, trying to do too many things at once can split your attention and make it harder to stay focused on the present. Instead, try single-tasking—focus on one activity at a time. Whether reading, working, or doing chores, give that task your full attention.

Engage in Activities that Keep You in the Now

Some activities naturally keep us engaged in the present moment. This could include physical activities like yoga, tai chi, or dancing, creative activities like painting or playing an instrument, or nature activities like gardening or hiking. Find activities that you enjoy and that help you stay focused on the here and now.

Use Mindful Reminders:

Set up small reminders to bring your focus back to the present. This could be a reminder on your phone, a note on your desk, or even a specific physical object. When you see this reminder, take a few moments to check in with yourself and refocus on the present.

Mindful Listening:

Practice listening fully in your interactions with others. Instead of thinking about what you'll say next or how what's being said affects you, listen. Notice the other person's words, tone of voice, and body language.

Grounding Techniques:

If you're feeling overwhelmed with anxiety or fear, use grounding techniques to help bring you back to the present. This could include techniques like the 5-4-3-2-1 method, where you identify five things you can see, four things you can touch, three things you can hear, two things you can smell, and one thing you can taste.

Remember, like any skill, this takes practice. Over time, these strategies can help you spend more time in the present moment, reducing anxiety, fear, and panic.

Lucy Pays Attention

In addition to cognitive restructuring, Lucy's therapist introduced her to mindfulness, a powerful therapeutic tool emphasizing being fully present at the moment and accepting one's feelings, thoughts, and bodily sensations without judgment. This was to help Lucy manage her anticipatory anxiety and curb her panic responses.

The therapist introduced Lucy to several mindfulness techniques. The first was mindfulness meditation, where she was taught to focus on her breath, noticing the sensation of inhaling and exhaling as a method of grounding herself in the present moment. Whenever her mind wandered to thoughts of driving or panic, Lucy was guided to gently bring her attention back to her breath.

Lucy was also taught the body scan technique, which involves bringing attention to different body parts from head to toe and noticing any sensations, discomfort, or tension. This was aimed at helping her develop a greater awareness of her body and better identify the physical signs of an impending panic attack, such as an increased heart rate or rapid breathing.

Another technique was mindful observation, where Lucy would focus on an object in her environment, such as a tree or a painting, and observe it in detail—its colors, texture, and form. This practice helped to anchor her attention in the present, keeping her mind from spiraling into panic-inducing thoughts.

The effect of these mindfulness techniques on Lucy's panic attacks was substantial. By learning to be fully present, she could recognize the onset of a panic attack early and intervene before it fully escalated. She became more adept at distinguishing between the physical sensations of a panic attack and actual physical harm, reducing the fear associated with these symptoms.

Furthermore, these mindfulness techniques helped reduce her anticipatory anxiety. By grounding herself in the present, she was less prone to fear-provoking thoughts about future panic attacks. This decreased her anxiety levels and made her less susceptible to panic attacks.

As for changes to Lucy's brain, regular mindfulness practice has improved the connectivity between her PFC (the brain's problem-solving center) and the amygdala (the brain's fear response center). As the connectivity between the amygdalofugal pathway and the uncinate fasciculus (two pathways that connect the amygdala and the PFC) is strengthened, her fear and stress responses are decreased. Furthermore, mindfulness can increase the density of the PFC, the area of the brain responsible for rational thinking and decision-making. As her PFC became more robust, she could better manage her fear and make rational decisions, like driving despite feeling anxious.

CHAPTER 5

COGNITIVE BEHAVIORAL STRATEGIES FOR ANXIETY MANAGEMENT

Understanding Cognitive Behavioral Therapy (CBT)

Cognitive behavioral therapy (CBT) is a form of psychotherapy that modifies dysfunctional emotions, thoughts, and behaviors by interrogating and uprooting negative or irrational beliefs. Considered a "solution-focused" approach to therapy, it aims to solve issues with practical, goal-oriented strategies. Cognitive behavioral therapy operates on the fundamental idea that our thoughts and perceptions influence our behavior.

Understanding CBT requires learning about the two key components of this therapeutic approach: cognitive therapy and behavioral therapy.

Cognitive therapy observes how negative thoughts or cognitions contribute to anxiety, depression, or other mental health disorders. Cognitive therapy aims to identify these negative thoughts and assess their validity. It seeks to change a person's thinking to be more adaptive and healthier.

Behavioral therapy focuses on the behavior itself and strives to identify harmful behaviors that are either a symptom or cause of the individual's psychological distress. It employs techniques to interrupt and eradicate these behaviors.

Cognitive behavioral therapy operates on the fundamental premise that our thoughts, feelings, and behaviors are intrinsically linked and that we can change how we feel by changing maladaptive thoughts and behaviors. Here's a more detailed look at how CBT works:

Assessment: The first step in CBT is typically a thorough assessment. This involves discussing their current difficulties, the history of these difficulties, and their impact on the client's life. The goal is to understand the problem and how it's affecting the individual's daily life and functioning.

Goal Setting: Based on the initial assessment, the therapist and client collaboratively set goals for therapy. Goals must be specific, measurable, achievable, relevant, and time-bound (SMART). They serve as a guide for the therapy process and a metric for evaluating progress.

Psychoeducation: Therapists provide clients with information about their symptoms and diagnosis to help them understand their condition. This includes explaining the CBT model and the interrelationship between thoughts, feelings, and behaviors. Understanding this model can empower clients, making them active participants in their recovery.

Cognitive Restructuring: This is a core technique used in CBT where clients learn to identify, challenge, and change unhelpful or distorted thoughts. It begins with identifying automatic negative thoughts in response to specific situations. Then, the client is taught to challenge these thoughts by evaluating their accuracy and usefulness. Finally, the client learns to replace these negative thoughts with more realistic and helpful ones.

Behavioral Interventions: This can include a range of techniques, such as exposure therapy for anxiety disorders, behavioral activation for depression, or role-playing to improve social skills. The goal is to help the client change maladaptive behaviors and learn more effectively.

Emotion Regulation: CBT can help clients learn strategies to manage and cope with intense emotional responses. Techniques include relaxation training, mindfulness, and distress tolerance skills.

Homework Assignments: Between sessions, clients are often given homework assignments to reinforce what was learned during therapy. This might involve practicing a new skill, challenging negative thoughts, or tracking behaviors and moods.

Relapse Prevention: Toward the end of therapy, a plan is made to maintain the gains from treatment and prevent relapse. This often involves identifying potential future challenges and creating a strategy for managing them.

Throughout all these steps, the therapeutic relationship is key. It's crucial for the therapist to build a strong rapport with the client and to provide a safe and non-judgmental space. Regular reviews of progress and collaborative decision-making are also important features of CBT. Remember, CBT is not a quick fix—it's a process that requires effort and active participation from the client.

Applying CBT Techniques to Anxiety, Fear, and Panic

Cognitive behavioral therapy uses various techniques to help manage and reduce feelings of anxiety, fear, and panic. The aim is to change the patterns of thinking or behavior causing a person's problems and, in turn, change how they feel. Here are some techniques commonly used:

Cognitive Restructuring or Reappraisal: One of the key techniques used in CBT to treat anxiety involves identifying and challenging irrational, negative beliefs and fears. The process involves:

- Identifying Negative Thoughts: The client is guided to become aware of specific thoughts that arise when they feel anxious or afraid.

- Challenging Negative Thoughts: Once these negative thoughts are identified, the therapist helps the client evaluate their validity and usefulness.

- Replacing Negative Thoughts: The client is then encouraged to replace irrational, negative thoughts with more positive, accurate, and beneficial ones.

Exposure Therapy: This method is particularly effective for phobias and obsessive-compulsive disorder (OCD). In exposure therapy, a person is gradually exposed to the situations or objects they fear in a safe and controlled environment. Over time, this exposure helps reduce the person's fear response.

Systematic Desensitization: This is often used alongside exposure therapy. It involves teaching the client relaxation techniques and having them imagine or confront anxiety-provoking situations while remaining calm. Over time, this helps desensitize them to these triggers.

Mindfulness and Relaxation Techniques: Techniques like deep breathing, progressive muscle relaxation, visualization, and mindfulness meditation can help people lower their overall daily anxiety levels and cope with stress, contributing to their ability to manage fear and anxiety when it arises.

Behavioral Activation: This technique is designed to guide clients toward engaging in enjoyable, fulfilling activities they might avoid due to anxiety. The goal is to lessen avoidance behaviors and increase experiences that bring pleasure and accomplishment, boosting mood and reducing anxiety.

Problem-Solving Therapy: This strategy helps people learn to manage the impact of stressful life events or situations that could contribute to anxiety. It involves identifying a problem, generating potential solutions, evaluating them, choosing a resolution to implement, and assessing the outcome. This approach can provide a sense of control and reduce feelings of anxiety.

Psychoeducation: This process involves teaching clients about their disorders and treatment, which can empower them to understand their symptoms, realize that their fears and anxieties are common, and work toward recovery.

Remember, therapy is a highly individual process, and these techniques would be tailored to the specific individual and their unique anxiety or fears. Also, it is common for therapists to combine these techniques as required, based on the individual's progress in therapy.

The Neuroscience Behind Why CBT Works

Neuroscience research has given us insights into why CBT can effectively manage anxiety. When people are exposed to threats or fearful situations, the amygdala, an area of the brain associated with emotions, becomes activated. This activation leads to physical anxiety symptoms such as a rapid heartbeat or sweaty palms.

Cognitive behavioral therapy is a form of treatment that focuses on examining the relationships between thoughts, feelings, and behaviors. It's a highly effective approach for various mental health conditions, including anxiety and depression. Neuroscience has begun to provide evidence to explain why CBT works. Here is a more detailed look at the neuroscience behind CBT:

Neuroplasticity and Learning

A fundamental principle behind the effectiveness of CBT lies in neuroplasticity—the brain's ability to reorganize itself by forming new neural connections throughout life. Neuroplasticity allows the brain's neurons (nerve cells) to compensate for injury and disease and adjust their activities in response to new situations or environmental changes, including therapeutic interventions like CBT.

Cognitive behavioral therapy is a form of learning. When you learn something, you form new or strengthen existing neural connections. In CBT, people learn new ways to think and behave. This learning reflects changes in neural pathways, especially in brain parts related to memory, learning, and emotion regulation, such as the PFC, hippocampus, and amygdala.

CBT and the PFC

The PFC, located at the front of the brain, is responsible for executive functions such as attention, self-control, decision-making, and emotional regulation. It's also involved in cognitive reappraisal, a key technique in CBT where individuals learn to identify and modify or reframe unhelpful thoughts or cognitive distortions.

In individuals with anxiety or depression, there is often hyperactivity in the amygdala, a brain area involved in fear response, and hypoactivity in the PFC. Cognitive behavioral therapy can help restore balance by reducing amygdala activity and enhancing PFC function, leading to better emotion regulation.

CBT and the Amygdala

The amygdala, an almond-shaped cluster of nuclei located deep within the brain, plays a key role in processing emotions and is particularly involved in the fear response. In conditions like anxiety disorders, the amygdala can become overactive, making individuals more reactive to perceived threats.

Cognitive behavioral therapy can help modulate the response of the amygdala. Techniques like exposure therapy, which involve facing fears in a safe and controlled environment, can decrease the fear response in the amygdala over time, reducing anxiety.

CBT and the Hippocampus

The hippocampus, located in the brain's medial temporal lobe, is crucial for memory formation. CBT can affect the hippocampus by strengthening the memory of new, healthier thoughts and behavior patterns. This is important for the long-term effectiveness of CBT, as it helps individuals remember and apply what they've learned in therapy even after treatment ends.

Neuroimaging studies have shown that CBT can increase hippocampus volume in individuals with PTSD and depression.

In conclusion, the effectiveness of CBT can be attributed to its ability to harness the brain's plasticity and capacity for learning and change. By targeting maladaptive thought patterns and behaviors, CBT can change neural pathways involved in emotion regulation, fear response, and memory, improving symptoms and overall mental health.

Changing Lucy's Mind, Part II

The therapist introduced Lucy to five cognitive behavioral strategies to help her move past her issues with anxiety, fear, and panic. Here are the five strategies.

Cognitive Restructuring: As discussed earlier, this strategy involves identifying and challenging fear-based, irrational thoughts.

To begin, the therapist worked with Lucy to help her understand the connection between her thoughts, feelings, and behaviors, explaining how negative thoughts can trigger emotional and physiological responses, leading to panic attacks.

Lucy was then encouraged to keep a thought diary to record her thoughts during anxiety or panic attacks, especially those related to driving. This exercise helped Lucy become more aware of her automatic negative thought patterns. For instance, she might jot down thoughts like *I'm going to crash,* or *I'm losing control,* which surfaced when she thought about driving.

Once these negative thoughts were identified, the therapist guided Lucy in challenging them. They examined each thought critically, assessing its validity and rationality. For example, the therapist asked questions such as, "What is the evidence that you will crash?" or "Have you lost control before while driving?" Lucy realized that most of these thoughts were not based on factual evidence but were distortions of reality fueled by fear.

Then came the phase of modifying or replacing these negative thoughts. The therapist worked with Lucy to find alternative, more realistic thoughts to replace her irrational ones. For instance, *"I'm going to crash,* could be replaced with *I've driven many times without crashing; I can do it again.* This step helped Lucy view driving as less threatening, consequently reducing her fear and anxiety.

Over time, as Lucy continued to practice cognitive restructuring, she began to see improvements. Her panic attacks became less frequent and less intense, and her fear of driving decreased. This transformative process was not instantaneous but took time, patience, and persistent practice. However, the continuous cycle of identifying, challenging, and replacing her negative thoughts gradually changed Lucy's fear-based thought patterns, enabling her to regain control over her life and reduce her panic attacks.

Exposure Therapy: This strategy involved Lucy gradually facing her fear of driving in a controlled and safe environment, with the goal of reducing her fear response over time. The therapist started with low-stress scenarios, such as sitting in a parked car, before gradually moving to more challenging tasks like driving around a parking lot and eventually driving on quiet streets.

Mindfulness Techniques: Lucy was taught several mindfulness techniques to keep her anchored in the present moment. These included mindfulness meditation, body scanning, and mindful observation. Regular practice of these techniques aims to reduce anticipatory anxiety and curb panic responses.

Relaxation Techniques: Relaxation techniques are crucial in managing anxiety and panic attacks. They help reduce the physiological arousal of panic and fear, such as a rapid heartbeat or shortness of breath.

Here are the specific relaxation techniques the therapist taught Lucy:

Deep Breathing: Often, during a panic attack, people breathe rapidly and shallowly from the chest, a style known as thoracic or chest breathing. The therapist taught Lucy to practice diaphragmatic, or deep breathing, which involves breathing from the diaphragm and expanding the belly instead of the chest. Deep breathing stimulates the body's relaxation response by slowing the heart rate and lowering blood pressure, countering the body's stress response. Lucy was taught to breathe deeply through the nose, hold for a few seconds, and then exhale slowly through the mouth.

Progressive Muscle Relaxation (PMR): PMR involves tensing and relaxing each muscle group in the body, usually starting from the toes and working up to the face. The goal is to create awareness of what tension and relaxation feel like in different body parts. This awareness can then spot and counteract the first signs of muscular tension that come with anxiety. The therapist guided Lucy through the process, instructing her to tense each muscle group for about five seconds and then relax for about thirty seconds before moving on to the next.

Visualization: This technique involves picturing a peaceful place or situation. Lucy was encouraged to imagine a serene location, like a beach or a meadow, detailing the sights, sounds, and smells of the place. By immersing herself in this calming scene, Lucy could reduce her anxiety and promote a sense of calm.

Mindfulness Meditation: Though a form of mindfulness, this technique also works as a relaxation tool. Lucy was taught to sit comfortably, close her eyes, and focus on her breath. The goal was to focus solely on breathing and bring her mind back to it whenever it wandered.

Yoga: While not directly taught in therapy, she was encouraged to explore yoga outside the therapy sessions. Yoga combines physical postures, breathing exercises, and meditation to reduce stress and promote relaxation.

Assertiveness training was an essential part of her therapy. Assertiveness, in this context, is the ability to express oneself and one's rights without violating the rights of others. It involves clear, open, and respectful communication. Assertiveness training was important for Lucy because anxiety often leads to passive or avoidant behaviors, which can further increase feelings of anxiety and helplessness over time.

The therapist started the assertiveness training by explaining the difference between passive, aggressive, and assertive behaviors to Lucy. Passive behavior often involves putting others' needs before oneself, not expressing personal feelings, or avoiding confrontation. On the other hand, aggressive behavior violates the rights of others and usually involves dominating others to get one's way. Assertive behavior strikes a balance between these two extremes. It involves expressing one's feelings, thoughts, and needs in a way that is respectful of both oneself and others.

After understanding these differences, Lucy was taught the steps to assertive communication. This included:

Clear, Non-Blaming Expression of Needs or Feelings: Lucy was taught to express her needs or feelings in a way that is direct, honest, and respects both her rights and those of others. For example, if she started feeling anxious when someone else was driving too fast, instead of staying silent out of fear of upsetting the driver, she was encouraged to say, "I'm feeling a bit anxious with the speed at which we're going. Could we slow down a bit?"

Use of "I" Statements: To avoid blaming or criticizing others, Lucy was encouraged to use "I" statements. Instead of saying, "You are driving too fast," which might make the other person defensive, she could say, "I feel anxious when the car goes this fast."

Active Listening: Assertiveness also involves listening actively to others. Lucy was encouraged to show that she was listening to the other person by using nonverbal cues, like nodding or maintaining eye contact, and verbal ones, such as paraphrasing or summarizing what the other person said.

Assertive Body Language: She was also coached on conveying assertiveness through her body language. This included maintaining eye contact, adopting an open posture, and speaking clearly and confidently.

Through role-playing exercises, Lucy practiced these assertive communication skills in therapy. This gave her the confidence to start applying them in real-life situations. By learning to communicate assertively, Lucy managed her anxiety better, as she could now express her feelings and needs effectively instead of bottling them up or avoiding situations that made her anxious. Over time, this assertiveness training played a key role in Lucy's journey to overcome her fear of driving and panic attacks.

CHAPTER 6

EMOTIONAL REGULATION AND SELF-CARE

The Science of Emotional Regulation

Emotional regulation refers to how individuals influence their emotions when they have them and how they experience and express these emotions. It's a complex process that involves initiating, inhibiting, or modulating one's state or behavior in each situation.

From a neuroscience perspective, emotional regulation involves several parts of the brain, but the PFC and the amygdala are critical.

<u>Amygdala</u>

The amygdala is part of the limbic system, which is responsible for emotions, survival instincts, and memory. It plays a crucial role in processing our emotions, especially fear and anxiety, and determines what memories are stored and where they are stored in the brain. It helps to set the emotional significance of a situation, and through connections with other parts of the brain, it helps coordinate the body's emotional response.

Prefrontal Cortex

The PFC, located at the front of the brain, is responsible for high-order cognitive functions, including decision-making, problem-solving, impulse control, and emotional regulation. The PFC can moderate the emotional reactions produced by the amygdala and respond with rational, controlled behavior. It does this by inhibiting the initial emotional response to reduce or prevent the intensity of the emotion being experienced.

Emotional Regulation Strategies

From a psychological perspective, emotional regulation strategies are divided into several types:

- **Cognitive Reappraisal** involves changing thoughts about a situation to decrease its emotional impact, for example, viewing a stressful event as a challenge rather than a threat.
- **Expressive Suppression** is an effort to hide or reduce outward expressions of emotion. For example, you are trying to keep a straight face when upset.
- **Distraction** involves shifting our attention from an emotional event to something less emotional.
- **Problem-Solving** involves identifying a problem causing emotional distress and then finding possible solutions.
- **Mindfulness** involves paying attention to the present moment, including emotions, without trying to change or judge them.

Recent research has shown that using the appropriate regulatory strategy in a given context or flexibly switching between strategies can be more beneficial for mental health than using any particular strategy.

Neuroplasticity and Emotional Regulation

The good news is that emotional regulation is a skill that can be improved with practice. This is thanks to neuroplasticity, the brain's ability to rewire itself and form new connections. Techniques such as mindfulness and CBT can help enhance emotional regulation skills, improve mood, and reduce anxiety.

Understanding emotional regulation and the brain regions involved gives us insight into our emotional responses and provides us with practical strategies to manage our emotions effectively.

Effective Self-Care Strategies for Anxiety Relief

Self-care can play a vital role in managing anxiety by helping maintain a healthy physical and mental balance, which is essential for overall well-being. Here's a deeper look at how self-care helps with anxiety relief:

Enhances Body Awareness: Regular self-care activities such as exercise or yoga promote awareness of your physical body. This awareness can make it easier to detect symptoms of anxiety early and take steps to manage them. Activities like yoga and meditation can help develop mindfulness, a skill crucial for anxiety management.

Promotes Relaxation: Self-care activities often promote relaxation and reduce stress. This relaxation can decrease the body's production of the stress hormone cortisol, which, in high amounts, can trigger or exacerbate anxiety.

Provides a Sense of Control: Regularly participating in self-care activities can give you control over your health and well-being. This sense of control can be incredibly beneficial for managing anxiety, which often stems from feeling a lack of control over situations.

Strengthens the Mind-Body Connection: Mindfulness, meditation, or yoga reduce stress and improve the mind-body connection. This improved connection can help you become more aware of the physical manifestations of anxiety and provide you with tools to address them.

Encourages Healthy Habits: Regular self-care can promote healthy habits such as regular exercise, good nutrition, and adequate sleep. These habits contribute to overall physical health, which is crucial for mental well-being. For example, physical activity releases endorphins (the body's natural painkillers and mood elevators) and promotes better sleep, which can help manage anxiety.

Builds Resilience: Regularly practicing self-care can build resilience over time, enhancing your ability to cope with stressors that can trigger anxiety.

Provides Distraction: Engaging in self-care activities can also serve as a distraction, preventing you from dwelling on anxious thoughts.

Fosters Self-Compassion: Self-care encourages a compassionate relationship with yourself. This self-compassion can be a powerful tool in managing anxiety, as it can help to reduce negative self-judgment, a common trait in people with anxiety disorders.

Effective self-care strategies can help manage anxiety symptoms and improve overall well-being. Here are some strategies that are particularly effective for relieving anxiety:

Regular Exercise: Physical activity is known to have various health benefits, including anxiety relief. Exercise triggers the release of endorphins, chemicals in the brain that act as natural painkillers and mood elevators. Try incorporating some form of exercise into your daily routine, whether a short walk, yoga, or more intense activities like running or cycling.

Healthy Eating: What you eat can significantly impact your feelings. Foods rich in magnesium (like leafy greens and legumes), zinc (like eggs and cashews), omega-3 fatty acids (like salmon and walnuts), and certain vitamins like B and D can help to reduce anxiety levels. Avoid excessive caffeine and sugar, which can spike your energy levels and crash them, leading to more anxiety.

Adequate Sleep: Sleep profoundly impacts your mood and emotional regulation. Lack of sleep can heighten anxiety and other mental health issues. Establish a regular sleep schedule, create a relaxing bedtime routine, and make your sleep environment comfortable and conducive to rest.

Mindfulness and Meditation: Mindfulness involves focusing on the present moment without judgment. This can be achieved through various techniques, including meditation, yoga, and deep-breathing exercises. Regular mindfulness practice can help reduce anxiety by breaking up negative thought patterns.

Social Connection: Spending time with friends and loved ones, talking to a trusted person about your feelings, or seeking support from online communities can help manage anxiety. Social connections can provide emotional support and distraction from worries.

Time in Nature: Spending time in natural environments can have a calming effect and reduce feelings of anxiety. This can involve hiking, picnicking in a park, or walking outside.

Limit Alcohol and Avoid Drugs: These substances can trigger or worsen anxiety and interfere with prescribed medication's effects.

Hobby and Leisure Activities: Engaging in enjoyable activities can distract you from anxiety and boost your mood. This could be anything from reading and gardening to painting or playing a musical instrument.

Journaling: Writing about your thoughts and feelings can be a therapeutic outlet for your worries and help you spot patterns and triggers in your anxiety.

Professional Help: If your anxiety feels overwhelming, it may be useful to seek professional help. A mental health professional can provide strategies and tools to help manage anxiety effectively.

It's important to remember that self-care looks different for everyone, and it's about what makes you feel nourished and cared for. Start with small changes and gradually incorporate more self-care activities into your routine. Please take note of the strategies that help you most and remember that it's okay to have days where you do less than others.

Restoring Balance: Sleep, Nutrition, and Exercise

Restoring balance in your life involves intentionally making changes to achieve a sense of equilibrium in your physical, mental, emotional, and social well-being. Sleep, nutrition, and exercise are crucial in managing and reducing anxiety. Here's why they are important:

Sleep: Adequate and quality sleep is essential for maintaining good mental health and managing anxiety. Lack of sleep can increase anxiety levels, impair cognitive function, and negatively impact mood regulation. On the other hand, sufficient sleep helps restore energy, supports emotional regulation, and improves overall well-being. A regular sleep routine and good sleep hygiene can promote better sleep quality and help alleviate anxiety symptoms.

Nutrition: Proper nutrition is essential for optimal brain function and emotional well-being. Certain nutrients, such as omega-3 fatty acids, vitamin B, magnesium, and zinc, have been linked to improved mood and reduced anxiety. On the other hand, a diet high in processed foods, sugar, and caffeine can contribute to increased anxiety and a disrupted mood. A balanced diet that includes whole foods, fruits, vegetables, lean proteins, and healthy fats can provide the nutrients needed for brain health and help regulate emotions.

Exercise: Regular physical activity has been shown to reduce anxiety significantly. Exercise releases endorphins, natural mood-boosting chemicals in the brain. It helps reduce stress, improves sleep, increases self-esteem, and enhances overall well-being. Engaging in aerobic exercises, such as walking, jogging, swimming, or dancing, for at least thirty minutes most of the week can greatly reduce anxiety symptoms.

In addition to these individual benefits, sleep, nutrition, and exercise also work synergistically to support mental health.

- Quality sleep improves cognitive function and emotional regulation, making it easier to make healthy dietary choices and engage in regular exercise.
- Proper nutrition provides the necessary fuel and nutrients for physical activity and improves sleep quality.
- Regular exercise can help improve sleep quality, increase appetite for nourishing foods, and boost mood and overall mental well-being.

By paying attention to sleep, nutrition, and exercise, you can establish a strong foundation for managing anxiety. These lifestyle factors contribute to your overall health and well-being, providing essential support in reducing anxiety symptoms and promoting a more balanced, resilient, and positive mental state. It's important to remember that individual needs may vary, and consulting with healthcare professionals can provide personalized guidance for optimizing sleep, nutrition, and exercise routines to support your anxiety management.

Restoring balance in these three areas is not an overnight fix but a gradual process. It's about making small, sustainable changes to your lifestyle that can significantly impact your mental health. With consistency, patience, and time, these changes can help to reduce anxiety and improve overall well-being.

Lucy Practices Self-Care

The therapist also taught Lucy various self-care strategies to manage her anxiety. Self-care practices are essential for maintaining mental health, as they help individuals manage stress, relax, and recharge. Here are the specific self-care strategies that she learned and began practicing daily:

Physical Exercise: Regular physical activity was strongly encouraged, as exercise releases endorphins (known as 'feel-good' hormones), helps regulate mood, and acts as a natural stress reliever. Lucy chose to take up jogging and yoga, which she found enjoyable and relaxing.

Healthy Diet: Lucy was advised to maintain a balanced diet of fruits, vegetables, eggs, and meat from organically raised animals. Foods high in vitamin B, like leafy green vegetables and beans, were suggested, as these can help reduce stress. She was also encouraged to limit caffeine, sugar, and alcohol, which can exacerbate anxiety and trigger panic attacks.

Sleep hygiene refers to practices and habits necessary for good sleep quality and full daytime alertness. Recognizing the importance of sleep for Lucy's overall well-being and anxiety management, the therapist emphasized the importance of maintaining good sleep hygiene. Here are the specific strategies Lucy learned and incorporated into her routine:

- Consistency: Lucy was advised to maintain a consistent sleep schedule. This meant going to bed and waking up simultaneously every day, even on weekends. This regularity helps regulate the body's internal clock, promoting better sleep.
- Bedtime Routine: Establishing a relaxing routine before bed was also important. Lucy was encouraged to develop calming pre-sleep rituals like reading a book, taking a warm bath, listening to soft music, or practicing deep breathing or relaxation exercises.
- Sleep-Optimized Environment: Lucy made her bedroom more conducive to sleep. This included keeping the room dark using curtains or an eye mask, keeping the temperature cool, and reducing noise with earplugs or a white noise machine. She also invested in comfortable mattresses and pillows.
- Screen Curfew: Lucy was advised to avoid screens like her phone, computer, or TV for at least an hour before bedtime. The blue light emitted by these devices can interfere with the production of the sleep hormone melatonin.
- Avoiding Large Meals, Caffeine, Sugar, and Alcohol: Consuming large meals, caffeine, sugar, or alcohol close to bedtime can disrupt sleep. Lucy started having her dinner a few hours before bedtime and limited her intake of caffeine, sugar, and alcohol, especially in the evening.
- Physical Activity: Regular physical activity can help promote better sleep. Lucy, who started jogging and doing yoga, was advised, however, to avoid vigorous workouts close to bedtime as they might make it harder to fall asleep.
- Use of Bed: Lucy was advised to use her bed only for sleep and sex. This helps the brain associate the bed with sleep and not with other activities that can cause alertness, stress, or anxiety.
- Mindfulness and Relaxation Techniques: If Lucy could not sleep because of anxiety, she was encouraged to use the mindfulness and relaxation techniques she learned in therapy. This could include deep breathing, progressive muscle relaxation, or visualization.

Mindfulness Practices: Lucy continued to use mindfulness techniques outside of therapy sessions. Mindfulness practices like meditation, deep breathing, or simply paying attention to her surroundings during a walk helped Lucy stay grounded in the present moment and prevent anxious thoughts about the future.

Social Connections: Strengthening social ties was another key self-care strategy. Spending quality time with friends and family, talking about her feelings with trusted individuals, and receiving their support benefited Lucy's mental well-being.

Leisure Activities: Lucy was encouraged to spend time each day doing something she enjoyed—a hobby, listening to music, reading, gardening, or anything else that brought her joy and relaxation. This helped distract her from her worries and provided a sense of accomplishment and satisfaction.

Journaling: Writing about her thoughts, feelings, and experiences daily helped Lucy understand her anxiety better. This practice also served as an emotional outlet, helping her articulate her fears and anxieties and reducing their intensity.

Self-Compassion: Lastly, Lucy was encouraged to practice self-compassion. This meant treating herself with the same kindness and understanding she would show a good friend, rather than being harsh or overly critical.

Self-compassion was a critical part of Lucy's recovery process and ongoing self-care practices. Practicing self-compassion involves treating oneself with kindness, understanding, and acceptance, especially in instances of perceived failure or suffering. It's about recognizing that everyone makes mistakes and experiences hardship, which doesn't have to result in self-criticism or harsh judgment.

Here's how Lucy began to practice self-compassion:

Self-Kindness *vs.* Self-Judgment: Lucy learned to be gentle and kind to herself, particularly when she was struggling with her anxiety or when a therapy session was challenging. Instead of blaming or criticizing herself when her anxiety levels rose or a panic attack occurred, she would tell herself things like, "It's okay. This is hard, and it's okay to struggle. I'm doing the best I can."

Common Humanity *vs.* Isolation: Lucy was reminded that she was not alone in her experience of suffering. Understanding that others experienced similar struggles helped her feel connected rather than isolated. She also began attending a support group for people experiencing anxiety and panic attacks, reinforcing this sense of common humanity.

Mindfulness *vs.* Over-Identification: Mindfulness, which Lucy had been practicing in therapy, was also an essential aspect of self-compassion. By practicing mindfulness, Lucy learned to observe her emotions of anxiety and fear without judgment and without getting swept up or overwhelmed by them. This allowed her to recognize when she was suffering, treat herself kindly, and respond appropriately.

Self-Compassionate Letter Writing: To help foster self-compassion, the therapist suggested Lucy write a letter to herself during a moment of calm, addressing a future situation where she might be anxious or experiencing a panic attack. In the letter, Lucy was kind and understanding, acknowledging her struggle, expressing care and support, and reminding her future self of her strength and resilience. This letter became a comforting tool she could return to in times of distress.

By learning and practicing self-compassion, Lucy was able to change the way she responded to her anxiety and panic attacks. Instead of spiraling into self-criticism or fear, she learned to comfort and care for herself, enhancing her emotional resilience and contributing significantly to her journey toward overcoming her panic attacks and anxiety.

By incorporating these self-care strategies into her daily life, Lucy managed her anxiety more effectively. These habits offered additional support alongside therapy, reinforcing the skills she learned during her sessions and promoting overall mental and emotional well-being.

CHAPTER 7

TECHNIQUES FOR EXPOSURE AND DESENSITIZATION

Understanding Exposure Therapy

Exposure therapy is a well-established and highly effective treatment approach used in psychotherapy to address anxiety disorders and phobias. It systematically and gradually exposes individuals to fearful situations, objects, or thoughts to reduce anxiety and fear responses. Here is a detailed explanation of exposure therapy:

Assessment and Planning: The therapist begins by conducting a comprehensive assessment to identify the specific fears, triggers, and avoidance behaviors related to the individual's anxiety. This assessment helps determine the appropriate exposure techniques and develop a tailored treatment plan.

Psychoeducation: The therapist educates the individual about anxiety and the rationale behind exposure therapy. They explain that avoidance and safety behaviors can maintain anxiety over time and that, through exposure, it is possible to learn that feared situations are not as threatening as perceived.

Fear Hierarchy: A fear hierarchy is collaboratively created, which is a ranked list of feared situations or stimuli. The hierarchy starts with situations that induce mild anxiety and gradually progresses to more anxiety-provoking situations. This allows for a step-by-step approach to exposure.

Imaginal Exposure: In cases where the fear is related to thoughts or memories, the individual is guided through imaginal exposure. This involves vividly imagining the feared situation or recalling traumatic memories in a safe environment. The goal is to confront and process the associated anxiety and distress.

In Vivo Exposure: In vivo exposure refers to facing feared situations or stimuli directly in real-life situations. The individual is gradually exposed to these situations, starting with the least anxiety-provoking ones from the fear hierarchy. They remain in the situation until their anxiety decreases, allowing them to learn that their feared outcomes do not occur.

Interoceptive Exposure: Interoceptive exposure involves deliberately inducing bodily sensations or physical symptoms associated with anxiety. This helps individuals confront and tolerate uncomfortable physical sensations, such as a rapid heartbeat or shortness of breath, often feared in anxiety disorders.

Extended Exposure: Extended exposure involves prolonged exposure to the feared situation or stimuli. The individual remains in the situation for an extended period until their anxiety naturally decreases. This helps break the avoidance cycle and teaches them that fear naturally subsides over time.

Response Prevention: During exposure therapy, individuals are encouraged to refrain from engaging in safety behaviors or avoidance strategies that typically temporarily relieve anxiety. They learn that fear naturally diminishes without these crutches by resisting the urge to escape or seek reassurance.

Gradual Progression: Exposure therapy follows a systematic and gradual progression, ensuring that individuals feel adequately prepared for each step. The individual's comfort level and readiness to face more challenging situations determine the pace.

Therapist Support and Guidance: Throughout the exposure process, the therapist provides guidance, support, and reassurance to help individuals manage their anxiety effectively. They help individuals challenge and reevaluate their fears, providing a safe and non-judgmental space for exploration and growth.

Exposure therapy is typically conducted over several sessions, and homework assignments are often given to practice exposure techniques between sessions. By repeatedly facing fearful situations and learning that anxiety naturally decreases, individuals can gradually reduce their avoidance behaviors, overcome anxiety, and regain control over their lives.

It is important to note that exposure therapy should be conducted by a trained mental health professional who can tailor the treatment to the individual's specific needs and ensure their safety and well-being throughout the process.

Systematic Desensitization

Systematic desensitization is a specific technique within exposure therapy used to treat anxiety disorders and phobias. It reduces anxiety by gradually exposing individuals to fearful situations or stimuli while teaching them relaxation techniques. Here is a detailed explanation of systematic desensitization:

Assessment and Planning: The therapist begins by assessing the specific fears, triggers, and avoidance behaviors related to the individual's anxiety. This assessment helps develop a tailored treatment plan for systematic desensitization.

Establishing a Fear Hierarchy: Together with the individual, the therapist creates a fear hierarchy, which is a ranked list of feared situations or stimuli. The hierarchy starts with the least anxiety-provoking situations and gradually progresses to the more anxiety-inducing ones. This allows for a step-by-step approach to desensitization.

Relaxation Training: Before exposing the individual to the feared situations, the therapist teaches relaxation techniques such as deep breathing, progressive muscle relaxation, or guided imagery. These techniques help the individual elicit a state of peace and counteract anxiety symptoms.

Exposure to Imagined Scenes: The individual is asked to imagine the least anxiety-provoking situation from the fear hierarchy while practicing relaxation techniques. They vividly visualize themselves in the feared situation and simultaneously relax to counteract anxiety. This process is repeated until the individual can imagine the situation without significant anxiety.

Gradual Exposure to Real-Life Situations: Once the individual has mastered relaxation in imagined scenes, they begin facing real-life situations corresponding to the fear hierarchy. Starting with the least anxiety-provoking situation, the individual enters the situation while employing relaxation techniques to reduce anxiety. They gradually progress to more challenging situations as they build tolerance and confidence.

Reinforcement and Gradual Progression: Throughout the process, the individual receives positive reinforcement and encouragement for their efforts and progress. The pace of progression through the fear hierarchy is determined by the individual's comfort level and readiness. The therapist ensures that each step is challenging but manageable for the individual.

Generalization and Maintenance: As the individual becomes more comfortable facing previously feared situations, the therapist helps them generalize their newfound confidence and coping skills to other similar situations. This promotes long-term maintenance of the desensitization effects beyond the therapy sessions.

Continued Practice and Support: Systematic desensitization often involves homework assignments for the individual to practice facing feared situations outside of therapy sessions. The therapist provides ongoing support, guidance, and feedback to ensure the individual's progress and address any challenges that may arise.

Systematic desensitization is a gradual and structured process that allows individuals to gradually confront their fears while learning relaxation skills to manage anxiety. The individual's anxiety response diminishes through repeated exposures and relaxation practice, and they develop a new association between the feared situation and relaxation rather than fear.

It's important to note that systematic desensitization should be conducted by a trained mental health professional who can tailor the treatment to the individual's specific needs and ensure their safety and well-being throughout the process.

The Neurobiology of Exposure and Desensitization

Exposure therapy and desensitization are two well-established techniques in the therapeutic arsenal against anxiety disorders, including phobias and panic disorders. To understand why these approaches work, delving into the neurobiology behind fear responses is essential. Here is a detailed explanation of the neurobiology of exposure and desensitization:

Fear Circuitry and the Amygdala: The amygdala, a key structure in the brain's limbic system, plays a central role in fear processing and emotional responses. When individuals encounter a feared stimulus or situation, the amygdala quickly activates, initiating the fear response. This activation triggers a cascade of physiological and cognitive processes associated with anxiety and fear.

Fear Extinction and the Prefrontal Cortex: Exposure therapy and systematic desensitization aim to promote fear extinction, which involves the weakening or suppression of fear responses. The PFC, particularly the ventromedial prefrontal cortex (vmPFC) and the medial prefrontal cortex (mPFC), plays a critical role in fear extinction. These areas regulate emotional responses and form inhibitory connections that help suppress the amygdala's fear response.

Neural Plasticity and Fear Memory Reconsolidation: Exposure and desensitization techniques leverage the brain's capacity for neural plasticity, which refers to its ability to reorganize its neural connections in response to experiences. Through repeated exposure to feared stimuli in a safe and controlled manner, new associations are formed, and fear memories can be reconsolidated.

Inhibition of Fear Responses: During exposure and desensitization, the repeated activation of the amygdala in response to feared stimuli leads to habituation and a decrease in fear responses. This occurs through inhibitory processes mediated by the PFC, which sends signals to dampen amygdala activity. Over time, this inhibitory control strengthens, reducing fear and anxiety.

Neurotransmitters and Neurochemical Changes: Exposure and desensitization techniques can change neurotransmitter levels and activity within the brain. For example, releasing gamma-aminobutyric acid (GABA), a neurotransmitter that inhibits neural activity, helps reduce anxiety and fear responses. Additionally, exposure therapy can modulate serotonin, norepinephrine, and endorphins, which are involved in mood regulation and the experience of pleasure and reward.

Neurocircuitry and Emotional Regulation: Exposure and desensitization techniques affect various interconnected brain regions of emotional regulation and fear processing. These include the amygdala, PFC, hippocampus, and insula. Through exposure and desensitization, these regions work together to recalibrate fear responses and establish new associations that promote a sense of safety and decreased anxiety.

Understanding the neurobiology of exposure and desensitization helps explain why repeated and controlled exposure to feared stimuli can lead to fear extinction and reduced anxiety responses. It highlights the brain's capacity for plasticity and adaptation, emphasizing the potential for individuals to reshape their fear responses and promote more adaptive patterns of emotional regulation.

It's important to note that the neurobiological processes underlying exposure and desensitization are complex and interconnected, and individual responses may vary. Mental health professionals trained in exposure-based therapies can utilize this knowledge to tailor treatment approaches and optimize the effectiveness of these techniques in reducing anxiety and promoting emotional well-being.

Lucy, Slowly and Gradually Loses Her Fears

The desensitization process Lucy undertook, guided by her therapist, involved systematic desensitization and exposure therapy. Systematic desensitization is a type of behavioral therapy that combines relaxation techniques with gradual exposure to anxiety-inducing stimuli or situations. Here's a detailed step-by-step process of how Lucy worked to desensitize herself to her triggers:

Establishment of a Hierarchical List of Fears: Lucy's therapist worked with her to create a hierarchy of anxiety-provoking situations related to driving, ranging from least to most anxiety-inducing. The list started with imagining herself in a car, then sitting in a parked car, eventually leading to driving on a quiet street, and finally, driving on a busy highway. This list serves as a roadmap for Lucy's therapy, providing a structured and progressive way for her to confront and manage her anxiety around driving. Here's a more detailed look at how Lucy and her therapist went about creating this hierarchy:

Identifying Fear-Provoking Situations: The therapist began by asking Lucy to identify all the situations related to driving that caused her anxiety or fear. She was encouraged to be as specific as possible. This included scenarios like being in a car, turning on the ignition, driving on a quiet street, or driving in heavy traffic.

Ranking the Situations: Once Lucy had a list of anxiety-provoking situations, the therapist asked her to rank these situations from least to most anxiety-inducing. For instance, just sitting in a stationary car might cause her Level 2 anxiety (on a scale of 10), while driving on a busy highway might cause Level 9 anxiety.

Creating the Fear Hierarchy: The therapist and Lucy worked together to structure this ranked list into a hierarchy. The aim was to create a gradual progression from the least anxiety-provoking to the most anxiety-provoking situations.

Here's an example of what Lucy's fear hierarchy might look like:

- Level 1: Imagine sitting in a parked car.
- Level 2: Actually sitting in a parked car.
- Level 3: Sitting in a car with the engine running but not moving.
- Level 4: Driving around an empty parking lot.
- Level 5: Driving on a quiet residential street.
- Level 6: Driving on a busier city street during non-peak hours.
- Level 7: Driving on a city street during rush hour.
- Level 8: Driving on a highway with light traffic.
- Level 9: Driving on a busy highway during peak hours.

Progression Through the Hierarchy: Once Lucy was comfortable with the first item on her hierarchy, she moved on to the next one. Lucy's therapist emphasized that this was a gradual process and there was no rush. It was more important that she felt in control and could manage her anxiety at each step.

Relaxation Techniques Mastery: Before initiating the exposure process, Lucy's therapist ensured that she was proficient in various relaxation techniques like deep breathing, progressive muscle relaxation, and mindfulness. The goal was to provide her with tools she could use to manage her anxiety during exposure to her triggers.

Imaginal exposure is a form of therapy where a person visualizes a fear-inducing scenario to gradually lessen the emotional impact of the feared situation. This technique is used to help people confront and manage fears or traumatic experiences that are not easily or safely accessible in real life.

In Lucy's case, the first step in the imaginal exposure process was selecting the least anxiety-inducing situation from her hierarchy of fears—imagining herself sitting in a parked car. Here's how the process unfolded:

Preparation: Lucy would start by finding a quiet, comfortable space where she wouldn't be disturbed. Her therapist would guide her through the process in their sessions, and she would practice independently at home.

Relaxation: Before beginning the visualization, Lucy would use the relaxation techniques she had learned. This could involve deep breathing exercises, progressive muscle relaxation, or mindfulness meditation. The aim was to start the exposure process calmly and relaxedly.

Visualization: Once relaxed, Lucy would begin to visualize the scenario. She would imagine herself sitting in a parked car, engaging as many senses as possible in her visualization to make it feel as real as possible. She would imagine the feel of the seat under her, the steering wheel in her hands, and the view through the windshield.

Anxiety Management: As she visualized the scenario, it was likely that Lucy would begin to feel some anxiety. When this happened, she was taught to acknowledge the anxiety without trying to push it away and then use her relaxation techniques to manage it. This might involve pausing the visualization to take deep breaths or reminding herself of her grounding techniques.

Repetition: This process of visualization and relaxation would be repeated multiple times within a single session and over many sessions until Lucy could visualize the scenario without feeling significant anxiety.

Reflection: After each imaginal exposure session, Lucy would have a chance to reflect on the experience with her therapist. They would discuss any anxieties and how well the relaxation techniques worked. These reflections would help them understand how she was progressing and plan for the next steps.

By repeatedly facing her fears in a controlled, imaginary context, Lucy gradually reduced her anxiety associated with the situation. The success of this stage would then set the groundwork for the next stage in her therapy: confronting the next anxiety-inducing situation in her hierarchy.

In Vivo Exposure: After Lucy became comfortable imagining the situations, in vivo (real-life) exposure was introduced. Again, starting with the least anxiety-provoking situation, she gradually began to confront her fears in real life while using her relaxation techniques to manage her anxiety.

This step was vital for Lucy to regain her confidence and reduce her driving anxiety. Here's a detailed look at how the in vivo exposure process worked:

Starting Small: The first step in Lucy's real-life exposure was the least anxiety-provoking situation from her fear hierarchy. Given her successful imaginal exposure practice, she was sitting in a parked car. She would sit in the car, allowing herself to acclimate to the environment without the additional stress of driving.

Applying Relaxation Techniques: While in the car, Lucy would practice the relaxation techniques she'd been taught. She would use deep breathing, progressive muscle relaxation, or grounding techniques if she felt any anxiety. Over time, this would help her associate the car environment with calmness and control rather than anxiety and fear.

Progressing Gradually: Once Lucy felt comfortable sitting in a parked car, she would move on to the next situation in her hierarchy, which might be starting the car engine or driving around an empty parking lot. Each progression would only occur when she felt ready and had demonstrated an ability to manage her anxiety at the current level.

Regular Practice: In vivo exposure, like any exposure therapy, requires frequent and consistent practice. Lucy was encouraged to repeat these steps regularly in and out of therapy sessions to reinforce her confidence and decrease her anxiety response.

Managing Setbacks: During in vivo exposure, it's natural to have days when anxiety feels overwhelming. The therapist reassured Lucy that setbacks were part of the process. Instead of being discouraged, Lucy was taught to see these moments as opportunities to practice her relaxation techniques and self-compassion.

Celebrating Success: Each step forward was celebrated, no matter how small it seemed. Completing each stage of the hierarchy was an achievement and a testament to Lucy's resilience and courage.

By going through this process, she could gradually expose herself to the situations that triggered her panic attacks and anxiety in a controlled and manageable way. This methodical approach allowed her to confront her fears in a safe environment, thereby reducing her anxiety over time and helping her regain the ability to drive without fear.

Regular Practice: Lucy was encouraged to practice these steps regularly during therapy sessions and on her own. Regular exposure helped Lucy become habituated to the situations that previously caused her anxiety and panic attacks.

Consistent and regular practice is crucial to the therapeutic process of overcoming phobias or anxiety disorders. It allows for repeated and reinforced exposure to the triggers, helping the brain to unlearn the fear response and replace it with a more manageable one.

In Lucy's case, the regular practice was two-fold:

Therapeutic Practice: Lucy and her therapist would go through her exposure exercises during her therapy sessions. The therapist provided guidance and immediate feedback, helping her fine-tune her approach to managing anxiety. These sessions also allowed for a review of 'her progress, identifying potential setbacks, and adjusting the therapeutic plan as necessary.

Home Practice: Equally important were Lucy's at-home practices. She was encouraged to repeat her exposure exercises outside of the therapy sessions. This could involve sitting in the car, driving short distances in low-stress environments, or simply visualizing the situations that caused her anxiety.

This regular practice aimed to accustom Lucy to the situations that triggered her panic attacks. Habituation is a psychological learning process whereby the intensity of emotional responses to a stimulus decreases over time with repeated exposure. For her, this meant that the more she faced the situations that caused her anxiety, the less anxious she would become. The regular practice provided the repeated exposure necessary for this habituation to take place.

Moreover, practicing these steps alone also helped Lucy build self-confidence and autonomy. It allowed her to realize that she could manage her anxiety independently, reinforcing her belief in her ability to control her panic attacks.

Lucy's therapist emphasized that consistent practice was more important than the speed of progression through the hierarchy. Everyone's pace is unique in therapy, and Lucy was reassured that her journey was about steady progress, not speed. This regular practice, combined with Lucy's commitment to the process, helped her decrease her anxiety and regain her ability to drive without fear.

Dealing with Setbacks: During this process, Lucy was taught to see any setbacks not as failures but as part of her journey. Anxiety can fluctuate, and some days might be harder than others. During these times, she was encouraged to apply self-compassion and continue her practice without self-judgment. Setbacks are not a sign of failure but a normal part of overcoming anxiety disorders. Here's how Lucy's therapist helped her navigate these challenges:

Normalizing Setbacks: Lucy's therapist first worked to normalize the experience of setbacks. Anxiety can fluctuate due to numerous factors, including stress, hormonal changes, a lack of sleep, etc. Some days might be more difficult than others, and that's okay. It doesn't mean Lucy is regressing or that therapy isn't working.

Reframing Perspective: The therapist helped Lucy reframe setbacks as opportunities rather than failures. Instead of seeing them as signs of an inability to cope, they were viewed as chances to better understand her anxiety triggers and to practice the coping skills she'd been learning. Each setback was a valuable learning experience that could inform her therapeutic process and help her build resilience.

Self-Compassion: Crucially, Lucy was taught to apply self-compassion during difficult times. Self-compassion involves being kind to oneself, recognizing that struggle is a part of the human experience, and maintaining a balanced perspective during challenging times. When she experienced a setback, she was encouraged to speak to herself as she would to a close friend going through the same situation, offering understanding and patience rather than criticism.

Continuing Practice Without Self-Judgment: Even when faced with setbacks, Lucy was urged to continue her exposure practice. Rather than judging herself harshly or getting stuck in negative thought patterns, she was encouraged to acknowledge her feelings and then refocus on her coping strategies. The goal was not to be always free of anxiety but rather to develop the skills to manage it effectively when it does occur.

Review and Adjust: Lucy and her therapist would review what happened in therapy sessions following setbacks. They'd discuss her feelings, thoughts, and reactions to better understand the setback. The goal was to extract lessons from the situation and adjust her therapeutic strategies as needed, promoting growth and resilience.

By adopting these strategies, Lucy could handle setbacks with resilience and continue her therapeutic journey. This approach helped her manage her panic attacks and anxiety around driving and equipped her with valuable skills for handling life's inevitable challenges.

Over time, through this systematic, step-by-step desensitization process, Lucy significantly reduced her anxiety related to driving. Her fear of experiencing a panic attack while driving lessened, and she regained control over her life, no longer needing to avoid driving due to fear.

CHAPTER 8

THE IMPACT OF LIFESTYLE ON ANXIETY AND FEAR

The Neuroscience of Exercise and Anxiety Management

Exercise has long been recognized as a powerful intervention for reducing anxiety and promoting overall mental well-being. In recent years, the field of neuroscience has shed light on the underlying mechanisms that contribute to the beneficial effects of exercise on anxiety management. This chapter explores the intricate relationship between physical activity and the brain, uncovering the neurobiological processes that occur during exercise and their impact on anxiety. By understanding the neuroscience of exercise, we can harness its potential to develop more effective anxiety treatment and prevention strategies.

Neurotransmitters and Mood Regulation

Serotonin: Serotonin is a neurotransmitter known for its role in mood regulation. Exercise has been shown to increase serotonin levels in the brain, promoting happiness and well-being. Activating serotonin receptors through exercise can have an anxiolytic effect, reducing anxiety symptoms and improving mood.

Dopamine: Dopamine is involved in reward processing and motivation. Exercise triggers the release of dopamine in the brain, leading to feelings of pleasure and motivation. The increase in dopamine levels during exercise can help alleviate anxiety by enhancing positive emotions and reducing stress.

Norepinephrine: Norepinephrine is a neurotransmitter that plays a crucial role in the body's stress response. Regular exercise can regulate norepinephrine levels, producing a more balanced stress response. This modulation of norepinephrine contributes to the anxiety-reducing effects of exercise.

Stress Response and Cortisol Regulation

HPA Axis: The hypothalamus–pituitary–adrenal (HPA) axis is a complex system in the body's stress response. Exercise has been found to regulate the HPA axis, leading to a more adaptive stress response. Regular physical activity helps to modulate cortisol, the primary stress hormone. Exercise can mitigate anxiety symptoms by reducing cortisol levels and improving the body's response to stress.

Endorphins: Exercise stimulates the release of endorphins, natural painkillers, and mood enhancers. Endorphins interact with opioid receptors in the brain, producing feelings of euphoria and reducing anxiety. These endogenous opioids significantly influence exercise's stress-reducing and mood-elevating effects.

Neuroplasticity and Structural Changes

Hippocampus: The hippocampus is a brain region involved in memory and emotional processing. Chronic stress and anxiety can lead to structural changes in the hippocampus, contributing to the persistence of anxiety disorders. Exercise has been shown to promote neurogenesis and increase the volume of the hippocampus. These changes enhance emotional regulation and improve the brain's ability to cope with stress and anxiety.

Amygdala: The amygdala is responsible for the fear response and plays a key role in anxiety. Exercise can reduce amygdala activity, resulting in a dampened fear response. This modulation of the amygdala helps to alleviate anxiety symptoms and promote a sense of calm.

Endocannabinoid System

Anandamide: Anandamide is an endocannabinoid involved in mood regulation. Exercise increases the production and release of anandamide, which can bind to cannabinoid receptors in the brain, promoting relaxation and reducing anxiety. The activation of the endocannabinoid system by exercise contributes to its anxiolytic effects.

Brain-Derived Neurotrophic Factor (BDNF)

Neuroplasticity and BDNF: Brain-Derived Neurotrophic Factor (BDNF) is a protein that supports the survival and growth of neurons. Exercise has increased BDNF levels in the brain, particularly in mood regulation and anxiety regions. Elevated levels of BDNF promote neuroplasticity, the formation of new connections in the brain, and the protection of existing neurons. This neuroplasticity contributes to improved mental health and anxiety management.

Conclusion

The neuroscience of exercise and anxiety management provides valuable insights into the neurobiological processes underlying the beneficial effects of physical activity on anxiety. By influencing neurotransmitters, stress response, neuroplasticity, and the endocannabinoid system, exercise offers an effective and natural approach to managing anxiety symptoms. Understanding these mechanisms enables us to develop targeted exercise interventions and optimize anxiety treatment strategies. Incorporating regular exercise into one's lifestyle can be a powerful tool for promoting mental well-being and enhancing anxiety management.

Nutrition and Mental Health

The connection between nutrition and mental health is a rapidly growing field of research that highlights the significant impact of diet on brain function and mental well-being. The food we consume provides the necessary nutrients for optimal brain health, and imbalances or deficiencies in certain nutrients can contribute to the development or exacerbation of mental health disorders. Here is a detailed explanation of the connection between nutrition and mental health:

Neurotransmitters facilitate communication between neurons (nerve cells) in the brain and other parts of the nervous system. They are chemical messengers that transmit signals across synapses, which are the junctions between neurons. Neurotransmitters are involved in various physiological processes and regulate a wide range of functions, including:

Transmission of Nerve Signals: Neurotransmitters enable the transmission of electrical impulses, or nerve signals, between neurons. When an electrical signal reaches the end of a neuron, it triggers the release of neurotransmitters from tiny sacs called vesicles. These neurotransmitters cross the synaptic gap and bind to specific receptors on the postsynaptic neuron, transmitting the signal and allowing it to propagate through the neural circuit.

Regulation of Mood and Emotions: Many neurotransmitters play key roles in regulating mood and emotions. For example:

Serotonin: Serotonin affects mood regulation, sleep, appetite, and social behavior. Imbalances in serotonin levels have been linked to depression, anxiety, and other mood disorders.

Dopamine: Dopamine is associated with pleasure, reward, motivation, and movement. It plays a role in regulating mood and motivation. Dysfunctions in dopamine signaling are implicated in addiction, Parkinson's disease, and schizophrenia.

Norepinephrine: Norepinephrine is involved in the body's stress response, attention, and arousal. It helps regulate mood and is associated with the fight-or-flight response.

Control of Motor Functions: Certain neurotransmitters, such as acetylcholine and dopamine, control motor functions and movement. They facilitate the communication between neurons in the brain's motor regions, allowing smooth and coordinated muscle movements.

Cognitive Functions: Neurotransmitters are essential for various cognitive functions, including learning, memory, and attention. For example:

Glutamate: Glutamate is the primary excitatory neurotransmitter in the brain and is involved in synaptic plasticity, learning, and memory formation.

Gamma-aminobutyric acid (GABA): GABA is the primary inhibitory neurotransmitter in the brain, acting to regulate and balance neuronal activity. It plays a role in reducing anxiety, promoting relaxation, and preventing excessive neural excitation.

Regulation of Autonomic Functions: Neurotransmitters also play a role in regulating autonomic functions, which are involuntary bodily processes. For example:

Acetylcholine: Acetylcholine regulates heart rate, digestion, and other autonomic functions.

Epinephrine (adrenaline) and norepinephrine: These neurotransmitters are released during the stress response and affect heart rate, blood pressure, and other physiological responses.

Omega-3 fatty acids, including eicosapentaenoic acid (EPA) and docosahexaenoic acid (DHA), are polyunsaturated fats essential for brain health and optimal brain function. Here is a detailed explanation of why omega-3 fatty acids are crucial for brain health:

Structural Component of Brain Cells: DHA is an integral structural component of brain cell membranes. The brain is highly enriched with fats, and DHA represents a significant proportion of the fatty acids in the brain. It helps maintain the fluidity and flexibility of cell membranes, allowing for efficient communication between brain cells. Adequate levels of DHA support the formation and maintenance of healthy brain cell structures, contributing to optimal brain function.

Neurotransmitter Function: Omega-3 fatty acids play a role in regulating neurotransmitter function in the brain. Neurotransmitters are chemical messengers that transmit signals between neurons, influencing mood, cognition, and behavior. Eicosapentaenoic acid and DHA help support neurotransmitters' production, release, and activity, including serotonin, dopamine, and norepinephrine. Adequate levels of these neurotransmitters are essential for mood regulation, cognitive processes, and overall mental well-being.

Anti-Inflammatory Properties: Omega-3 fatty acids possess anti-inflammatory properties, and chronic inflammation has been associated with various neurological conditions, including depression, anxiety, and neurodegenerative diseases. Eicosapentaenoic acid and DHA can help modulate inflammatory processes in the brain, reducing inflammation and oxidative stress. Doing so helps protect brain cells from damage and promotes a healthy inflammatory response, which is crucial for maintaining brain health.

Synaptic Plasticity and Neuroprotection: Synaptic plasticity refers to the ability of synapses (connections between neurons) to adapt and change in response to experiences and learning. Omega-3 fatty acids, particularly DHA, support synaptic plasticity, allowing for optimal neuronal communication and the formation of new connections in the brain. This process is crucial for learning, memory, and cognitive function.

Furthermore, omega-3 fatty acids have been shown to exhibit neuroprotective properties. They help protect brain cells from oxidative stress, reduce neuronal inflammation, and enhance the brain's resistance to damage.

These neuroprotective effects may contribute to preventing or slowing down age-related cognitive decline and the development of neurodegenerative disorders.

Mental Health and Emotional Well-Being: Research suggests that omega-3 fatty acids, particularly EPA, play a role in supporting mental and emotional well-being. Adequate intake of omega-3s has been associated with a reduced risk of depression, and supplementation with EPA has shown positive effects in reducing symptoms of depression and other mood disorders. Omega-3 fatty acids may help regulate neurotransmitter function, reduce inflammation, and support overall brain health, all of which contribute to improved mental health outcomes.

Conclusion: Omega-3 fatty acids, specifically EPA and DHA, are essential for brain health and function. They contribute to the structural integrity of brain cells, support neurotransmitter function, possess anti-inflammatory properties, promote synaptic plasticity, and offer neuroprotection. Adequate intake of omega-3 fatty acids through diet or supplementation is crucial for maintaining optimal brain health, cognitive function, and emotional well-being.

Micronutrients and antioxidants are important for promoting mental health and managing anxiety. Here is a detailed explanation of why these compounds are beneficial for anxiety:

Neurotransmitter Balance: Micronutrients, such as vitamin B, zinc, and magnesium, are essential for the production and regulation of neurotransmitters in the brain. Imbalances or deficiencies in these micronutrients can disrupt neurotransmitter function, contributing to anxiety symptoms. For example:

Vitamin B (B6, B12, and folate) are involved in synthesizing and metabolizing neurotransmitters like serotonin, dopamine, and GABA, which play crucial roles in mood regulation and anxiety management.

Zinc regulates the GABA system, which has calming effects on the brain and helps reduce anxiety.

Magnesium helps regulate the HPA (hypothalamic-pituitary-adrenal) axis, which is involved in the body's stress response. Adequate magnesium levels can help modulate stress and anxiety responses.

Reduction of Oxidative Stress: Anxiety is associated with increased oxidative stress, which occurs when there is an imbalance between the production of reactive oxygen species (ROS) and the body's antioxidant defense mechanisms. Antioxidants help neutralize ROS and reduce oxidative stress. Micronutrients such as vitamins C and E, selenium, and beta-carotene act as antioxidants, protecting brain cells from oxidative damage and potentially decreasing anxiety symptoms.

Regulation of Inflammation: Chronic inflammation has been linked to anxiety and mood disorders. Micronutrients, particularly antioxidants, can help modulate inflammation in the body and brain. For example:

Vitamins C and E, as well as other antioxidants, have anti-inflammatory properties and can help reduce inflammation that may contribute to anxiety.

Omega-3 fatty acids, which possess anti-inflammatory effects, can help regulate the immune system and reduce inflammation in the brain, potentially alleviating anxiety symptoms.

Energy Production and Stress Regulation: Micronutrients, including vitamin B, are essential for energy production and metabolism in the brain. Adequate energy levels are crucial for proper brain function and stress regulation. Vitamin B, such as B5 and B12, helps support adrenal function and the production of stress hormones. By promoting optimal energy metabolism and stress regulation, these micronutrients can contribute to anxiety management.

The gut–brain axis is a bidirectional communication system that connects the gastrointestinal tract (the gut) with the brain and the central nervous system. It involves a complex network of biochemical signaling pathways, neural connections, and the influence of the gut microbiota (the collection of microorganisms residing in the digestive system). This axis allows for ongoing communication and interaction between the gut and brain, influencing various physical and mental health aspects.

The gut–brain axis operates through multiple mechanisms:

Neural Pathways: Direct communication occurs through the vagus nerve, which connects the brainstem to various organs in the body, including the digestive system. The vagus nerve carries signals from the gut to the brain and vice versa, allowing bidirectional communication and influence between these two systems.

Neurotransmitters and Hormones: The gut produces and releases neurotransmitters and hormones that can influence brain function and behavior. For example, serotonin, a neurotransmitter associated with mood regulation, is primarily produced in the gut. Additionally, hormones such as ghrelin and leptin, involved in appetite regulation, can impact brain activity and feelings of hunger or satiety.

Immune System Activation: The gut has a large population of immune cells and is involved in immune system function. Immune cells in the gut can release inflammatory cytokines and other signaling molecules that can affect the brain. Chronic inflammation in the gut can contribute to systemic inflammation, potentially impacting brain health and mental well-being.

Microbiota Influence: The gut microbiota, composed of trillions of microorganisms such as bacteria, fungi, and viruses, plays a significant role in the gut–brain axis. The gut microbiota can produce neurotransmitters, metabolites, and other bioactive compounds that influence brain function and behavior. They can also interact with the immune system and control inflammation, affecting brain health.

The gut–brain axis has profound implications for various aspects of health:

Mental Health: The gut–brain axis has been strongly linked to mental health conditions such as anxiety, depression, and stress-related disorders. Alterations in gut microbiota composition, increased gut permeability (leaky gut), and imbalances in neurotransmitters and hormones can contribute to these conditions.

Cognitive Function: The gut–brain axis can influence cognitive function, including memory, attention, and learning. Factors such as gut inflammation, microbiota diversity, and the production of certain neurotransmitters can impact cognitive processes.

Appetite and Food Intake: The gut–brain axis regulates appetite, food intake, and satiety. Signals from the gut, including hormones and neurotransmitters, can influence feelings of hunger and fullness, affecting food choices and eating behaviors.

Stress Response: The gut–brain axis is involved in the regulation of the stress response. Stress can impact gut health, alter gut microbiota composition, and disrupt the balance of neurotransmitters and hormones in stress regulation.

Understanding and modulating the gut–brain axis holds promise for developing interventions targeting mental health conditions and other disorders. Strategies such as dietary modifications, probiotics, prebiotics, and other gut-directed therapies are being explored to optimize gut-brain communication and promote overall well-being.

Conclusion: Micronutrients and antioxidants are crucial in promoting mental health and managing anxiety. They contribute to neurotransmitter balance, reduce oxidative stress, regulate inflammation, support energy production and stress regulation, and influence the gut–brain axis. Adequate intake of these compounds through a balanced diet or supplementation can help support overall brain health, reduce anxiety symptoms, and improve emotional well-being. However, it is important to note that while nutrition can support anxiety management, it should be part of a comprehensive approach that includes professional guidance and other appropriate treatments.

The Role of Sleep in Anxiety Management

Sleep plays a crucial role in anxiety management, and sleep disruptions can contribute to developing and exacerbating anxiety symptoms. Here is a detailed explanation of the role of sleep in anxiety management:

Emotional Regulation: Adequate sleep is essential for emotional regulation. When well-rested, our brains are better equipped to process and regulate emotions effectively. Sufficient sleep supports the PFC, responsible for rational thinking, decision-making, and emotional regulation. Inadequate sleep, on the other hand, can impair these functions, making it more challenging to manage anxious thoughts and emotions.

Anxiety Threshold: Sleep deprivation lowers the threshold for experiencing anxiety. It makes individuals more vulnerable to perceiving situations as threatening or stressful, leading to heightened anxiety responses. Adequate sleep, on the other hand, helps maintain a higher threshold for anxiety, enabling individuals to cope better with stressors and manage anxiety symptoms.

Cognitive Functioning: Sleep is vital for cognitive functioning, including attention, memory consolidation, and problem-solving abilities. Anxiety can interfere with these cognitive processes, and insufficient sleep can exacerbate these deficits. By getting enough quality sleep, individuals can enhance their mental functioning and maintain clearer thinking, enabling them to manage anxiety-inducing situations better.

Stress and Cortisol Regulation: Sleep and stress are closely interconnected. Chronic stress and anxiety can disrupt sleep patterns, leading to difficulties falling asleep, staying asleep, or experiencing restorative sleep. Lack of sleep, in turn, can exacerbate the stress response and increase levels of the stress hormone cortisol. Elevated cortisol levels can contribute to heightened anxiety and a reduced ability to cope with stress. Establishing healthy sleep patterns helps regulate cortisol levels, supports stress management, and reduces anxiety.

Sleep–Wake Cycle and Circadian Rhythms: Sleep is regulated by the sleep–wake cycle and circadian rhythms, which are influenced by the natural light–dark cycle. Disruptions to these rhythms, such as irregular sleep schedules or exposure to artificial light at night, can impact sleep quality and quantity. Irregular sleep patterns can disrupt the balance of neurotransmitters and hormones involved in mood regulation and anxiety, potentially leading to increased anxiety symptoms. Maintaining a consistent sleep schedule and practicing good sleep hygiene help support the synchronization of the sleep–wake cycle and promote healthy circadian rhythms, facilitating better anxiety management.

Restorative Function: Sleep is essential for restoring and repairing the body and mind. During sleep, the brain undergoes processes that support neural regeneration, memory consolidation, and the removal of waste products. Adequate sleep provides an opportunity for the brain to recover from daily stressors and restore its optimal functioning. By ensuring sufficient and restorative sleep, individuals can enhance their resilience to anxiety and improve their overall mental well-being.

In summary, sleep plays a critical role in anxiety management. Adequate and quality sleep supports emotional regulation, raises the threshold for anxiety, enhances cognitive functioning, regulates stress responses, synchronizes circadian rhythms, and facilitates the restoration of the mind and body. Prioritizing good sleep habits and addressing sleep disturbances can significantly reduce anxiety and mental health.

Lucy Makes Lifestyle Changes

Lifestyle changes can play a pivotal role in managing anxiety. For Lucy, these modifications were about reducing panic attacks while driving and supporting her overall mental health. Here's a detailed look at the lifestyle changes Lucy implemented:

Physical Activity: Regular exercise reduces anxiety and improves mood by boosting endorphin production in the body. Lucy incorporated exercise into her routine, starting with walks and gradually introducing strenuous activities like running or yoga. This physical activity provided a healthy outlet for her anxiety and enhanced her overall physical health.

Healthy Eating: Nutrition also plays a significant role in mental health. Lucy started making conscious food choices, choosing a balanced diet rich in fruits, vegetables, lean proteins, and whole grains. She also limited her caffeine and sugar intake, which can exacerbate anxiety symptoms.

Sleep Hygiene: Quality sleep is essential for emotional regulation and stress management. Lucy focused on improving her sleep hygiene. She established a regular sleep schedule, created a peaceful sleep environment, and incorporated relaxation techniques like progressive muscle relaxation or mindful breathing before bedtime.

Mindfulness Practices: Lucy introduced mindfulness exercises into her daily routine. These exercises, like mindful breathing or mindful eating, helped her stay present and prevented her from worrying about the future.

Self-Care Routines: Lucy is committed to practicing self-care regularly. This could be as simple as taking a relaxing bath, spending time in nature, reading a book, or pursuing a hobby. These activities provided her with a respite from anxiety and helped her maintain a positive mindset.

Reducing Alcohol Consumption: Alcohol can interfere with the effectiveness of CBT techniques and exacerbate anxiety. Lucy decided to limit her alcohol consumption as part of her lifestyle change.

Maintaining a Support Network: Lucy worked on maintaining her relationships with her friends and family and building new supportive relationships. These connections provided emotional support and gave her opportunities for relaxation and enjoyment.

Time Management: Lucy practiced better time management to prevent stress from over-commitment or last-minute rushes. She learned to prioritize her tasks, delegate when possible, and set aside time for relaxation and self-care.

Lucy created a healthier and more balanced daily routine through these lifestyle changes. These changes and her ongoing therapy significantly helped her manage her anxiety and panic attacks, contributing to her overall well-being and quality of life.

CHAPTER 9

BUILDING RESILIENCE AND FOSTERING POSITIVE CHANGE

Understanding Resilience from a Neuroscientific Perspective

Resilience is a complex process involving multiple brain areas and various neurological mechanisms. Understanding resilience from a neuroscientific perspective can help us understand how some people can effectively cope with stress and anxiety while others might struggle.

Here are a few key points about resilience from a neuroscientific perspective:

Neuroplasticity: One of the central concepts in neuroscience is the brain's plasticity, its ability to adapt and change in response to experiences, learning, and damage. This is a critical factor in resilience. Individuals with greater neuroplasticity may be better equipped to recover from stressful events and adjust their behavior to reduce anxiety.

Amygdala and Hippocampus: The amygdala and hippocampus are two key brain areas involved in anxiety and resilience. The amygdala is involved in emotional processing and is particularly important for fear responses. On the other hand, the hippocampus plays a significant role in learning and memory, especially contextual and spatial memories. When a person faces a stressor, the amygdala signals a threat, while the hippocampus helps contextualize the danger based on past experiences. Individuals with a resilient brain show better regulation of the amygdala, meaning less overactivity in response to stress, and better hippocampus functioning, allowing for a more accurate interpretation of stressful events.

Prefrontal Cortex (PFC): The PFC plays a key role in executive functions such as decision-making, emotional regulation, and inhibitory control. It helps us analyze and interpret stressful events and decide how to respond. People with more resilient brains tend to have a more active PFC during times of stress, which helps them regulate their emotions, consider various options, and resolve problems.

Neurotransmitters and Hormones: Stress and anxiety influence the levels of various neurotransmitters and hormones in the brain. For instance, the stress hormone cortisol is often elevated in people under chronic stress. However, those with high resilience can maintain a balanced cortisol response, which helps prevent the harmful effects of chronic stress. Similarly, neurotransmitters such as serotonin, dopamine, and norepinephrine, associated with mood regulation, are modulated differently in resilient individuals.

Neural Connectivity: How different areas of the brain communicate with each other also plays a role in resilience. In people with high resilience, there's typically stronger connectivity between the PFC and the amygdala, allowing them to better regulate their emotional responses to stress.

The brain's ability to adapt to stress, regulate emotions, and make decisions in stressful situations are key resilience factors. Understanding these processes can lead to interventions that enhance resilience and reduce anxiety. It's important to remember that resilience is also influenced by many other factors outside of the brain, including genetics, environment, personal experiences, and learned coping strategies.

Strategies for Building Resilience

Building resilience for managing anxiety involves cultivating habits and skills that promote positive adaptation to adversity or stress. Here are several strategies that can help build resilience:

Cognitive behavioral therapy (CBT) helps you identify and change thought patterns that lead to harmful behaviors or emotional distress. It's an evidence-based approach that's been found effective for anxiety and many other mental health conditions.

Mindfulness and Meditation: Regular mindfulness practice can help increase your ability to tolerate distress, manage stress, and regulate emotions. Techniques such as focused breathing, progressive muscle relaxation, and mindfulness-based stress reduction (MBSR) can be helpful.

Physical Activity: Regular exercise can help manage anxiety symptoms by reducing levels of the body's stress hormones, such as adrenaline and cortisol. It also stimulates the production of endorphins, the body's natural mood elevators.

Healthy Eating: Good nutrition supports brain health. A balanced diet can help regulate mood and energy levels, contributing to overall well-being and resilience.

Adequate Sleep: Poor sleep can contribute to anxiety, while sufficient sleep can enhance problem-solving skills and help regulate emotions. Good sleep hygiene practices, such as establishing a consistent sleep schedule and creating a comfortable sleep environment, can improve the quality of your sleep.

Positive Relationships: Social support is crucial for resilience. Building strong, positive relationships with friends, family, and community members can provide emotional support during stressful times.

Problem-solving Skills: Develop and practice good problem-solving skills. Assessing and addressing problems as they arise effectively reduce anxiety and enhances resilience.

Gratitude Practice: Cultivating an attitude of gratitude can shift your focus from negative or stressful thoughts to positive ones. This can be done through activities like keeping a gratitude journal.

Positive Affirmations: Positive self-talk and affirmations can help you manage stress and foster resilience. They can help you maintain a positive outlook and overcome negative thought patterns.

Professional Help: If anxiety becomes overwhelming, don't hesitate to seek professional help. A mental health professional can provide support and guidance, helping you to build resilience and cope with anxiety.

Remember, building resilience is a process, not a destination. It involves personal growth and learning, and it takes time. Be patient with yourself as you develop these new habits and skills.

Embracing Positive Change: Embracing positive change when dealing with anxiety involves recognizing and challenging negative thought patterns, developing a proactive attitude, and cultivating habits that promote mental well-being. Here are a few strategies:

Reframe Your Thinking: How you think about anxiety and change can greatly impact your feelings. Cognitive behavioral therapy (CBT) can help you identify and challenge negative thoughts and replace them with more positive, balanced beliefs.

Embrace Uncertainty: Much of the anxiety around change comes from the fear of the unknown. Instead of seeing uncertainty as threatening, try to view it as an opportunity for growth and learning.

Set Realistic Goals: Goals provide a sense of direction and purpose. Ensure your goals are S.M.A.R.T (Specific, Measurable, Achievable, Relevant, and Time-bound) to keep you motivated and focused.

Practice Mindfulness: Mindfulness allows you to be present in the moment and accept it without judgment. It can help you stay calm amidst change, reducing feelings of anxiety.

Develop Coping Strategies: Healthy coping strategies, such as regular exercise, adequate sleep, and good nutrition, can help manage anxiety and promote overall well-being.

Seek Support: Don't hesitate to seek support from trusted friends, family members, or a mental health professional. Having someone to share your thoughts and feelings with can make a big difference.

Embrace Personal Growth: Recognize that change is part of life and crucial to personal growth, even when challenging. Each challenge presents an opportunity to learn and become stronger.

Express Gratitude: Regularly expressing gratitude can help shift your focus from negative or stressful thoughts to positive ones. Try keeping a gratitude journal or taking a few minutes each day to reflect on what 'you're thankful for.

Learn Relaxation Techniques: Techniques such as deep breathing, progressive muscle relaxation, or yoga can help reduce anxiety and promote a sense of calm.

Stay Positive: Cultivate an optimistic outlook. This 'doesn't mean ignoring reality, but acknowledging the challenges while recognizing your abilities and resources.

Remember, it's normal to feel anxious when faced with change. How you manage this anxiety determines your ability to embrace positive change.

Be patient with yourself, and remember that it's okay to seek help if you need it.

Lucy Builds Resiliency

Building resilience, or adapting well to adversity, was a key part of Lucy's therapeutic journey. Resilience isn't something you're born with, but it can be built and cultivated. Here's a detailed look at the resilience-building strategies Lucy practiced:

Reframing Negative Thoughts: Cognitive restructuring played a significant role in helping Lucy build resilience. She was taught to identify and challenge negative or unhelpful thoughts, replacing them with more realistic, balanced views. This helped her avoid getting caught up in pessimistic thought patterns that could exacerbate her anxiety and fear.

Building Emotional Awareness: Lucy learned to understand and recognize her emotional responses. This involved identifying signs of anxiety and panic early on, giving her a better chance of managing these feelings effectively. Emotional awareness was cultivated through practices like mindfulness and journaling.

Strengthening Coping Skills: Lucy worked on building a toolkit of effective coping strategies, such as relaxation techniques, grounding exercises, and mindfulness practices. Regularly practicing these skills strengthened her ability to manage anxiety and panic, bolstering her resilience.

Establishing a Support Network: Lucy was encouraged to lean on her support network—friends, family, and her therapist—for help. Sharing her struggles and victories, asking for advice, or simply spending time with people who cared about her were all ways of fostering resilience.

Self-Care Practices: Prioritizing physical health and well-being through regular exercise, a balanced diet, and sufficient sleep supported Lucy's emotional resilience. She also made time for activities that she enjoyed and that helped her relax, boosting her mood and providing a break from stress.

Setting Realistic Goals: Lucy and her therapist worked together to set achievable, gradual goals for her exposure therapy. Achieving these goals, however small, boosted Lucy's confidence and fostered a sense of capability, reinforcing her resilience.

Fostering Self-Compassion: Lucy was taught to practice self-compassion, treating herself with kindness and understanding during difficult times. This approach helped her maintain a balanced perspective, avoid harsh self-criticism, and foster resilience.

Embracing Setbacks as Learning Opportunities: As part of her resilience-building, Lucy learned to view setbacks not as failures but as opportunities for growth and learning. This mindset shift helped her bounce back from challenges and continue progressing in her therapeutic journey.

By consistently practicing these strategies, Lucy built resilience—an invaluable asset not just for her specific situation but for handling life's challenges in general. This resilience, combined with the other skills and techniques she learned in therapy, empowered her to regain control over her anxiety and panic attacks and reclaim her freedom to drive without fear.

CHAPTER 10

CREATING YOUR ANXIETY MANAGEMENT PLAN

Creating an anxiety management plan involves understanding your triggers, knowing how to cope during anxious times, and taking steps to manage your overall mental health. Here's a step-by-step guide to creating an anxiety management plan:

Identify Triggers: Identify situations, places, or thoughts that trigger your anxiety. This could be anything from public speaking to deadlines at work, social events, certain thoughts, or fears.

Identifying triggers for anxiety can be an important step in managing it effectively. A trigger is anything that causes an increase in anxiety symptoms. These triggers can be external, such as being in a specific place or situation, or internal, such as a thought or physical sensation. Here are some steps to help you identify your anxiety triggers:

Keep a Journal: This is a practical way to identify your triggers. Every time you feel anxious, write down what you're doing, where you are, who you're with, what you're thinking about, and how you feel physically. Over time, you may start to see patterns or common factors that seem to be associated with your anxiety.

Reflect on Past Experiences: Think about times you've felt particularly anxious. Can you identify any common elements? For example, you might realize that you often feel anxious when you're in crowded places or when you have a lot to do.

Notice Your Physical Symptoms: Anxiety often manifests physically, with symptoms such as a rapid heartbeat, sweating, or feeling shaky. If you notice these or other physical symptoms of anxiety, note what's happening at that moment. This can help you identify triggers.

Consider Your Fears: What are you afraid of? Sometimes, anxiety triggers are closely tied to our fears. For example, if you have a fear of rejection, you might find that you feel anxious when you're anticipating a social situation.

Look at Your Lifestyle: Factors like your diet, sleep habits, and level of physical activity can all influence anxiety. If you notice that your anxiety seems worse when you're tired, for example, it could be that lack of sleep triggers it.

Get Professional Help: If you're having trouble identifying your anxiety triggers or if your anxiety feels overwhelming, it can be helpful to seek the support of a mental health professional. They can work with you to identify your triggers and develop a plan for managing your anxiety.

Remember that everyone's experience with anxiety is different, so what triggers anxiety for one person might not trigger it for another. Also, just because you've identified a trigger doesn't mean you need to avoid it. The goal is to learn how to manage your response to triggers, which can involve a range of strategies such as relaxation techniques, CBT, medication, and others.

Develop Coping Strategies: Once you've identified your triggers, the next step is to develop coping strategies for anxiety. These can include deep breathing, mindfulness meditation, progressive muscle relaxation, or other relaxation techniques.

Develop coping strategies for anxiety and panic attacks is crucial to managing these conditions. These strategies aim to help you manage your symptoms, navigate stressful situations, and reduce the frequency and intensity of anxiety and panic attacks. Here are a few coping strategies that can help:

Deep Breathing: This is a simple yet effective strategy. Deep, controlled breathing can help slow your heart rate, lower your blood pressure, and provide a focus other than your symptoms during an attack.

Grounding Techniques: These strategies help you stay connected to the present moment. They can include techniques like identifying and focusing on the physical details of an object nearby, naming what you see around you, or focusing on bodily sensations like the feeling of your feet on the ground.

Progressive Muscle Relaxation (PMR): This technique involves tensing and releasing different muscle groups. It can help you relax and distract your mind from the symptoms of a panic attack.

Mindfulness and Meditation: Mindfulness involves focusing on the present moment without judgment, while meditation is a practice that helps you relax and focus inward. Both can effectively manage anxiety and reduce the frequency of panic attacks.

Cognitive Behavioral Therapy (CBT): It helps you identify and change negative thought patterns that contribute to anxiety and panic attacks. This can be especially useful for learning to recognize and alter the thoughts that often trigger these attacks.

Lifestyle Adjustments: Regular exercise, a healthy diet, adequate sleep, and limiting caffeine and alcohol can all help reduce anxiety and the occurrence of panic attacks.

Support Network: Having a network of supportive friends and family can be extremely beneficial. You can turn to them when you're anxious or after a panic attack, and they can provide comfort and reassurance.

Professional Help: Don't hesitate to seek professional help if your anxiety or panic attacks become overwhelming. Therapists and psychiatrists can provide additional strategies and treatments, such as medication.

Exposure Therapy: Exposure therapy can be very beneficial if you have specific phobias that trigger anxiety or panic attacks. Under the guidance of a mental health professional, you gradually expose yourself to the fear-inducing situation until it no longer causes an extreme anxiety response.

Self-Care: Make sure to take time for relaxation and activities that you enjoy. This can help reduce overall stress and anxiety levels.

It's important to remember that everyone's experience with anxiety and panic attacks is different, and what works for one person may not work for another. Finding the best coping strategies for you may take some trial and error, and that's okay. Be patient with yourself, and remember to celebrate your progress, no matter how small it may seem.

Create a Routine: Regular exercise, adequate sleep, and a balanced diet can all contribute to reduced anxiety levels. Try to create a daily routine that includes these elements.

Include Relaxation Techniques: Regularly practice relaxation techniques such as mindfulness, yoga, or meditation. These can help reduce symptoms of anxiety and promote a sense of calm.

Write Down Positive Affirmations: Positive affirmations can help change negative thought patterns that may contribute to anxiety. Write down affirmations that resonate with you and read them regularly.

Have a Plan for Panic Attacks: If you experience panic attacks, include a specific plan for dealing with them. This can include a grounding technique, such as focusing on your breath or the physical sensations of an object you're holding, a specific relaxation technique, or a plan to contact a supportive person.

Stay Connected: Don't isolate yourself. Maintain contact with supportive friends and family members, and consider joining a support group for people with anxiety. Social support can make a big difference in managing stress.

Include Professional Support: If your anxiety is severe or self-help strategies aren't enough, include professional support in your plan. This can consist of therapy, such as CBT, or medication.

Regularly Review and Revise Your Plan: Your anxiety management plan should not be static. Periodically review it to see what's working and what needs to be improved. Revise your plan as necessary.

Remember that everyone's experience with anxiety is different, so what works for one person might not work for another. Finding what works best for you may take some trial and error. And don't hesitate to seek professional help if you need it. Mental health professionals can provide guidance and resources to help you manage your anxiety.

Implementing and Evaluating Your Plan

Creating an anxiety and panic attack management plan is one thing, but implementing and evaluating it is essential to ensuring it effectively addresses your needs. Here's how to go about it:

Implementation

Commitment: Commit to your plan and make it a part of your daily routine. This might involve setting aside time daily for relaxation techniques, taking prescribed medication, or performing physical exercise.

Flexibility: Understand that it's okay to adapt your plan as you go. You might find that some techniques are more effective than you'd hoped or that others work better than you expected.

Patience: Change takes time. Don't be discouraged if you don't see immediate results. Keep going, and remember that progress may be slow, but any progress is good.

Support: Enlist the help of supportive friends, family, or mental health professionals. They can provide encouragement, help you stay accountable, and offer guidance when needed.

Evaluation

Regular Check-Ins: Regularly assess your progress. You might want to keep a journal to track changes in your anxiety levels or the frequency of panic attacks. Over time, you should start to see patterns or improvements.

Feedback: Ask for feedback from people you trust. They can provide valuable outside perspectives on how you're doing.

Professional Input: If you're working with a mental health professional, they can provide expert insight on your progress and suggest any necessary adjustments to your plan.

Adjustments: You may need to adjust your plan based on your evaluation. A certain technique isn't working for you, or maybe you've found a new one you want to try. Be flexible and open to change.

Remember, creating, implementing, and evaluating a management plan for anxiety and panic attacks is a personal and ongoing process. What works for one person may not work for another, and that's okay. Most importantly, you're addressing your anxiety and improving your quality of life. Be patient with yourself, celebrate your progress, and don't hesitate to seek professional help if you need it.

Here's a sample anxiety and panic attack management plan. Everyone's experience with anxiety and panic attacks is different, so this plan may need to be tailored to your needs.

Objective: Manage anxiety and reduce the frequency and intensity of panic attacks.

Action Plan

Identify Triggers: Keep a journal for a month, noting when anxiety or panic attacks occur, what you're doing, where you are, who you're with, what you're thinking about, and how you feel physically.

Use this information to identify patterns and triggers for your anxiety and panic attacks.

Coping Strategies

Deep breathing: Practice breathing techniques for five minutes twice daily and use them when feeling anxious or experiencing a panic attack.

Mindfulness and meditation: Engage in mindfulness exercises for ten minutes daily, progressively increasing to twenty minutes over time.

Progressive Muscle Relaxation (PMR): Use PMR when you feel a panic attack coming on. Practice PMR exercises twice a week to become comfortable with the process.

Cognitive Behavioral Therapy (CBT): Book an appointment with a therapist for CBT sessions. Use the techniques learned during sessions when anxiety levels rise.

Lifestyle Changes

Regular exercise: Aim for thirty minutes of moderate-intensity exercise five days a week.

Balanced diet: Work with a nutritionist to create a diet plan that emphasizes whole grains, lean proteins, fruits, and vegetables and minimizes processed foods.

Adequate sleep: Aim for seven to nine hours of sleep per night. Establish a regular sleep schedule and create a comfortable sleep environment.

Social Support: Stay connected with supportive friends and family. Schedule regular catch-ups or phone calls.

Consider joining a support group for people with anxiety and panic disorders.

Professional Help: If self-help strategies aren't enough, consider seeing a psychiatrist for medication evaluation and management.

Continue CBT with a licensed therapist.

Evaluation

Monthly Check-Ins: Every month, review your journal to track your progress. Are you experiencing anxiety or panic attacks less frequently? Are they less intense when they do occur?

Therapist Feedback: Discuss your progress with your therapist during therapy sessions. They can provide valuable insight and suggest modifications to your plan if needed.

Adjustments: Make necessary adjustments to your plan based on your monthly check-ins and therapist's feedback. This could involve adding new coping strategies, modifying your lifestyle, or seeking professional help.

Managing anxiety and panic attacks takes time, and progress might be slow. Be patient with yourself and celebrate every success, no matter how small. Always contact a healthcare professional if your symptoms worsen or become unmanageable.

Lucy's Treatment Plan

Here is a detailed CBT treatment plan for Lucy with long-term goals and specific objectives.

Overall Treatment Goal: To help Lucy manage her anxiety, reduce the frequency and intensity of her panic attacks, and eliminate her fear of driving.

Objective 1: Identify and understand the triggers for Lucy's panic attacks.

Record and analyze panic attacks in a journal, noting the circumstances and thoughts associated with each episode.

Use this information to identify common triggers or patterns.

Objective 2: Teach Lucy cognitive restructuring techniques to change her negative thoughts.

Identify and challenge irrational or overly negative thoughts.

Replace these with more realistic, balanced perspectives.

Objective 3: Use exposure therapy to help Lucy confront and reduce her fear of driving.

Develop a fear hierarchy related to driving.

Use systematic desensitization to gradually expose Lucy to feared situations, starting with the least anxiety-provoking.

Progress from imaginal exposure to in vivo (real-life) exposure.

Objective 4: Develop and strengthen Lucy's coping strategies for managing anxiety and panic.

Teach Lucy relaxation techniques, such as deep breathing and progressive muscle relaxation.

Practice mindfulness exercises to help Lucy stay present and focused rather than getting caught up in worry or fear.

Train Lucy in assertiveness skills to help her express her needs and boundaries effectively.

Objective 5: Help Lucy build resilience to better handle setbacks and challenges.

Normalize the experience of setbacks, explaining that they are a normal part of the therapeutic process.

Teach her to view setbacks as learning opportunities rather than failures.

Foster self-compassion, encouraging her to treat herself with kindness and understanding during difficult times.

Objective 6: Encourage lifestyle changes that support anxiety management and overall mental health.

Help Lucy develop a regular exercise routine and a balanced diet.

Improve her sleep hygiene to ensure she gets quality rest.

Teach her self-care strategies, including regular relaxation and leisure activities.

Objective 7: Support Lucy in maintaining and expanding her social support network.

Encourage her to share her experiences and progress with trusted friends and family.

Explore opportunities for her to build new supportive relationships, such as by joining a support group or participating in community activities.

Relapse Prevention Plan

A key part of Lucy's treatment is creating a relapse prevention plan. This plan is designed to help Lucy identify potential triggers for relapse, take proactive steps to prevent it, and manage any instances of relapse effectively.

Objective 1: Identify potential triggers for relapse.

Continue the practice of recording and analyzing episodes of anxiety or panic, even as their frequency and intensity decrease.

Use this information to identify potential triggers for relapse.

Objective 2: Develop strategies for avoiding or managing identified triggers.

Use cognitive restructuring techniques to manage negative thoughts or feelings associated with potential triggers.

Practice relaxation and mindfulness techniques to manage immediate stress or anxiety related to these triggers.

Plan for handling high-risk situations (e.g., driving in heavy traffic or at night), such as using deep breathing exercises, having a support person present, or scheduling these activities at less anxiety-provoking times.

Objective 3: Create a clear plan for responding to early signs of relapse.

Identify early signs of relapse (e.g., increased anxiety, more frequent negative thoughts, and avoidance of driving).

Plan specific actions to take when these signs are detected, such as scheduling an extra therapy session, increasing the practice of relaxation and mindfulness exercises, or reaching out to supportive individuals.

Objective 4: Normalize and plan for potential setbacks.

Explain that relapses or setbacks are a common part of the recovery process and do not signify failure.

Reinforce the concept of self-compassion and treat setbacks as opportunities for learning and growth.

Plan for handling setbacks, including reassessing and adjusting the treatment plan, increasing the frequency of therapy sessions if needed, and providing additional support.

Objective 5: Maintain lifestyle changes that support mental health and reduce the risk of relapse.

Continue a regular exercise routine, a balanced diet, and good sleep hygiene.

Maintain regular self-care activities and relaxation practices.

Continue maintaining and expanding the social support network.

Incorporating this relapse prevention plan into Lucy's overall treatment will provide her with a clear strategy for managing her recovery over the long term. Regular reviews of this plan will be scheduled to ensure it remains effective and relevant to her ongoing progress.

Regular therapy sessions will be scheduled to provide ongoing support, monitor Lucy's progress, and adjust the treatment plan as needed. With this plan, the therapist aims to empower her with the skills and techniques to manage her anxiety effectively and regain her freedom to drive without fear.

CONCLUSION

In conclusion, *NeuroMastery: Retraining Your Brain to Conquer Anxiety, Fear, and Panic Attacks* is a comprehensive guide that educates readers about the fundamental dynamics of the brain and how they impact our response to anxiety-provoking situations. It provides a scientific understanding of anxiety, fear, and panic responses and offers actionable strategies and techniques grounded in neuroscience and psychology. Combining knowledge about the brain's anatomy and functions with effective cognitive behavioral and mindfulness practices gives the readers the tools to manage their anxiety and rewire their brain's response to fear. This book, therefore, serves as a significant resource for anyone looking to regain control over their emotional states and lead a more peaceful, resilient life.

NeuroMastery: Retraining Your Brain to Conquer Anxiety, Fear, and Panic Attacks goes beyond a simple self-help guide. It illuminates the underlying neurobiological processes that shape our emotional responses and provides a well-rounded, scientific understanding of anxiety, fear, and panic reactions. It delves into the brain's inner workings, explicating the roles of various neural structures like the amygdala, hippocampus, and PFC in fear processing and response. The book helps readers understand that their anxiety symptoms are not a personal failing but a manifestation of their brain's survival mechanisms.

The book then transitions from theory to practice. It introduces cognitive behavioral strategies that are well-established in the therapeutic field for their effectiveness in treating anxiety disorders. These strategies include cognitive restructuring, identifying and challenging irrational thoughts, assertiveness training, and exposure therapy. Each technique is described in detail, guiding readers through implementing it in their lives. These strategies aim to equip individuals with practical tools to interrupt the maladaptive anxiety responses their brain has learned over time.

Furthermore, the book highlights the transformative power of mindfulness. It provides step-by-step instructions for mindfulness exercises, explaining how these practices can help individuals foster a non-judgmental awareness of their thoughts and feelings, thereby reducing the intensity of anxiety and panic responses. It explains how consistent mindfulness practice can lead to neural changes, particularly in brain areas responsible for fear response and emotion regulation, effectively helping to rewire the brain's reaction to anxiety-provoking situations.

In addition to these strategies, the book emphasizes the importance of self-care routines, including maintaining good sleep hygiene, regular physical activity, and balanced nutrition, explaining how these lifestyle factors contribute to overall mental health and resilience.

NeuroMastery: Retraining Your Brain to Conquer Anxiety, Fear, and Panic Attacks offers a multidimensional approach to managing anxiety. Combining neuroscientific knowledge with practical therapeutic strategies empowers readers to take active steps toward reshaping their brain's fear responses. Consequently, it is a significant resource for anyone seeking to master their anxiety and cultivate emotional resilience, leading them toward a more peaceful and fulfilling life.